OU

OUT OF BOUNDS

The radical rehabilitation

of a converted ex-convict

Judith Wigley

Highland Books

GODALMING
SURREY

First published in 1992 by Highland Books, Two High Pines, Knoll Road, Godalming, Surrey, GU7 2EP. Second edition 1996.

British Library Cataloguing-in-Publication Data. A catalogue record for this book is available from the British Library.

ISBN: 1 897913 36 2

Printed in Great Britain by Caledonian International Book Manufacturing Ltd, Glasgow.

CONTENTS

Acknowledgments

I am deeply grateful to Malcolm for giving me the opportunity to write this very special story. It was my privilege. But my gratitude extends to the whole Worsley family–Jennifer, Helen and Paul–for allowing me to share in their lives both individually and corporately as a family. Their openness, honesty and patience throughout the period of research and writing will not be forgotten. Neither will the friendship, fellowship and fun that we've had together as families.

My special thanks go to the many people, too many to name, who took time to recall their memories and experiences of working with Malcolm; in particular, the ex-members of the Lindley Lodge community in Nuneaton.

My thanks to Sue Rosseter and Jim Heaton for their reading of the manuscript and correction of numerous spelling errors! I remain indebted to my special friends who have been constant in prayer throughout and who I know would not wish to be named.

Last but not least, I thank my children for allowing me to work through the early mornings of their 1991 summer holiday!

Judith Wigley

Foreword

Just occasionally you meet a person whose story, when it is told to you, is so gripping and remarkable that you know, even as you listen to it pouring out, that it is going to remain a living part of your own heart and mind permanently. Malcolm Worsley is one of that rare band of people whose account of his life has had that kind of effect on me.

When he came into my study in Coventry and we got talking and I invited him to tell me something of the experience which is the subject of this book, I was completely gripped by it. It wasn't until we had been talking for some time that I realised that I was, in fact, the second Bishop of Coventry to receive a blessing from this man. The first was my great predecessor, Bishop Cuthbert Bardsley, who, when Malcolm came to see him in this same study and told him something of the same testimony, actually physically gave him his blessing. Whereupon, Malcolm spontaneously returned the compliment, as you will read in the book. No wonder Bishop Cuthbert was absolutely delighted! For me also it was a joy to hear Malcolm and then pray with him.

I am delighted that now Malcolm's story has been so clearly, vividly and effectively put into writing by the wife of a vicar who played a key part in its unfolding. I am certain it will have the same vital effect on all those who read it that it has had on me. This is essentially a description of how a person can be remade by the grace of God. We often hear and talk about Jesus Christ having the power to change people's lives, 'If anyone be in Christ he is a new creation, a new being' (2 Corinthians 5:17). Many of us know, at least to some extent, that this has been true in our own lives. But it does something amazing for our faith and for our whole hope and expectation of what God can bring about in ourselves and in others when we read a book like this, the record of someone whose whole character and nature has been so obviously and totally renewed and redeemed.

The first sentences of this book find Malcolm re-entering the same prison he first arrived at as an inmate, now to be a member of its staff. Between those two entries lies a quite extraordinary change. A whole new world has truly come into existence. As we enter into the story, in the way in which its author, Judith Wigley, and its subject, Malcolm Worsley, have enabled us to do, we will find that we ourselves are profoundly affected by it. Do we really want God to help us to change? Do we really believe God can help us? Could the same miracle occur in our own lives as so manifestly comes to pass in the life of this seemingly helpless and hopeless figure, as he is when we first meet him in these chapters? It is the account of a miracle of healing and of transformation taking steady, convincing effect. The grace of God which grasps and transforms Malcolm comes to him through the word of God, the Bible which Max Wigley first puts into his hand. It comes to him in the solitude of his cell, meeting him in his inmost being on his own. It is profoundly moving to read of his astonishing ministry to his fellow prisoners, some of whom became disciples with him. God's grace also comes to him through the community and people of Christ. It comes first through the Vicar himself, Max Wigley, through Will Barker, his prison visitor, through Lindley Lodge and the team and community there, through St James, Weddington, and Guy and Helen Cornwall-Jones; and so through many in Nuneaton and in the Diocese of Coventry. Above all it comes to him through that remarkable helpmeet and partner, Jennifer, who truly suffers and grows with Malcolm as he comes into the fullness of his ministry to the homeless, the drop-outs, the victims of society, so needy then as now-and eventually to youngsters on probation and prisoners. There are so many points at which this grace restores and renews and heals not only Malcolm, but those to whom he is sent, even those whom earlier in his life he had injured. There is more to touch us and to convict us and to move us on every page as we go on to the end of this part of the story. And I can assure you that when you meet Malcolm now, the power of that grace reaches out through him to touch you afresh. I believe and hope that this tale will have a freshly converting influence upon whoever picks it up and begins to read. I am certain it will be a blessing to many, bishops included! I dare to pray that it will help significantly in bringing about the fundamental change in our own hearts and lives, and in the life of our church and society, which we desperately need today.

+Simon Coventry

One

Out Of Bounds

It was the first day of Malcolm Worsley's new job at Haverigg Prison. Walking along a narrow corridor in search of his new office, he reached a door. On it, was a sign which read OUT OF BOUNDS. Somewhat puzzled by the message he turned and retraced his steps back towards the entrance he had just left. He felt so sure that this was the correct, and only, route to his office. 'Obviously not', he told himself, 'there must be another way that I don't know of.' No sooner had the thought crossed his mind than he realised what he had done.

Ten paces from the door with his back to the sign he stood absolutely still, hardly daring to breathe. His body felt paralysed. Somewhere in the distance a voice was shouting, 'Malcolm, Malcolm, you have just walked away from a sign intended for a *prisoner*'. It was loud and repetitive, but some time before the words made any sense. When they did a terrifying uncertainty came over him. Who was he and what was he doing in this place? Confused and bewildered he realised that this was turning into one of the most traumatic moments of his life.

'Stop it, pull yourself together, why now, why now?' he said over and over again, in an attempt to regain control of his now trembling body. After all it wasn't the first time he had returned to Haverigg since that unforgettable departure nearly twenty years earlier. His last post, based in Whitehaven with Cumbria Probation Services had brought him here on many occasions to visit clients who were serving sentences inside Haverigg. Some of those visits had been recent. But today was definitely different.

His appointment as probation officer to Haverigg Prison had changed things considerably and the fact that he was here to stay hit him hard. It wasn't a fleeting visit of an hour or two that he could brace himself for, knowing full well that he'd be able to walk away until the next time, perhaps weeks or even months later. Today was the beginning of a much longer sentence. Every morning he would walk through the gates, past security and into the administration department. Every day he would face what had, a long time ago, been his nightmare. There was no running away from the past. Right now he knew he was reliving the nightmare and it was hurting. Somebody had opened the floodgates and Malcolm was drowning in a swamp of painful memories. Yes, he had been a convicted criminal and Haverigg had been his prison.

It wasn't the sight of the building that had gripped him, he was familiar enough with that. No, it was the sudden reminder of what life here had been like and the effect it had had on him as a person. Even though twenty years had passed since his last sentence, it was the old Malcolm that confronted him now. What little dignity and self worth he'd managed to salvage through the early years of life had been well and truly squashed in places of this kind. A prison sentence was the removal of rights, the restraint of all freedom. But for Malcolm it had been much more than that. Years of being locked up had suppressed parts of him to the point of destruction. He remembered it all too clearly.

Haverigg was category C, a semi-open prison. There were no small cells, heavy doors and great bundles of keys as in Armley, Risley, Liverpool, Wormwood Scrubs and so many of the others he had experienced. The dormitories, recreation facilities and industrial work rooms were meant to create a less restrained environment but the result for him was quite the reverse. Every waking moment was controlled and regimented by the presence of prison officers. Locked in a cell, you could at least kid yourself that you were locking the system out and retain some degree of privacy for part of the day. But here you were under observation twenty four hours a day living in fear of being 'nicked' for walking too fast, having a shoe lace untied, breathing too heavily, or having the wrong expression on your face. Or at least at times, it felt that way. The consequences of such 'sins' were severe and to be avoided at all costs. Allowances and rations could be forfeited, extra work duties enforced; but the ultimate in the old days was three days in the 'chokey block' in solitary with just bread and water to keep you alive. Each time you went down a part of you never returned; it was a long-drawn-out execution.

Once 'inside' you became a number, a nobody. You ate, slept, worked and exercised when told to. Even the timing of going to the loo was dictated by prison officers. There was no space for personality or individuality. The memories were deeply ingrained in Malcolm, and some experiences still hurt when he recalled them. Not even twenty years of rebuilding and restoring his life had fully removed the deep psychological damage of these prison years. Some memories, like the following incident at Wormwood, haunt him to this day.

It was a new sentence. As usual he was petrified but more so this time because it was Wormwood – and London. He had heard many tales about the prison and its inmates, none of which had given cause for encouragement. Big-time criminals, hardened prison officers and the vastness of the whole institution made him feel physically sick. With no letters to receive, no one to write to and certainly no hope of visitors, he didn't know if he'd survive the sentence.

Prison wages weren't issued in those days: just tobacco and match allowances when the work was completed. They became the lifeline of many new convicts like Malcolm whose nerves were well and truly frayed. As usual his first task was to scrub the cell floor. In desperation for the small quantity of tobacco that would make up two, perhaps three, cigarettes he slaved away until the grain in the wooden floor stood out. It was worth every ounce of energy for the release that the tobacco would bring to his shattered nerves.

Allowances were issued after the midday meal and so it was with great eagerness that Malcolm returned to his cell that lunchtime. The sight that faced him still troubles him to this day. Written in thick black wax (used by prisoners for waxing the thread on post office sacks) and sprawled across the cell floor in large bold capital letters were the words 'THIS IS FILTHY'. There was no tobacco, no matches - just a bucket and scrubbing brush and the instructions to do it again. It was a kick in the face, stomach and groin – all in one blow. It was a violent assault upon the spirit of a helpless man who now lay distraught in a quivering, blubbering heap upon the cell floor. A prison officer looked on, revelling in the sight. His mission had been accomplished.

That day in Wormwood felt like yesterday, not twenty or thirty years ago. How could he walk through the door, past the sign that had so suddenly removed the last twenty years from his life. The pain, the struggle, the stigma should have been behind him, yet here he was responding as an inmate. He wanted to pinch himself in the hope that he'd wake up from what had been just a bad dream; but, no, this was a living night-mare. There had been other crises over the years, hurdles to jump or knock down but none as devastating as this moment. Malcolm's two lives, past and present, had collided in the most extraordinary way.

He wasn't sure if he had the energy to fight, some-thing that he had grown accustomed to doing. The most he could manage was a cry from the heart, 'O God, help!' He stood for what seemed an eternity wondering if he would ever move again. Gradually a calm came over him and the words of the prison officer who released him from Haverigg at the end of his seventh and final sentence came into his mind: 'You'll be back Worsley, I know your type. You'll be back'. 'Yes', he said quietly to himself, 'I am back. He was right'. It wasn't in the manner expected but Malcolm Worsley was back inside Haverigg Prison. Perhaps there had been a purpose in this moment after all.

Twenty years had passed and with them a series of unbelievable events, not least the invitation from the prison governor to take up this very position, bringing him to this point. He had status and authority given to him by the prison service, and he had every right to walk through those doors.

Humbled and yet quietly confident in the God who had turned his life upside down, he lifted his head, turned slowly, and walked back down the corridor, through the door, past the sign and into his office.

Two

Life On The Run

The journey from Preston to Bradford was a well-worn route for Malcolm, and he felt sure that he could have driven it blindfolded. Tonight he needed to do just that. He ached all over from large, inflamed bruises that spread across his body; and his face throbbed with the pain of several breaks in the jawbone. His shoulder was badly dislocated.

It was just twenty four hours since he had discharged himself from hospital. What should have been at least a week's stay turned out to be only a day. Within that time doctor's had implanted wire into his face to hold the jaw bone together in the hope that it might heal. Eating had become a physical impossibility, and his mouth opened just far enough to get a drinking straw between his lips. The slightest movement resulted in excruciating pain. Nursing staff pleaded with him to stay, knowing there was a high risk of infection in the wound and explaining just how critical it was that the wire was removed at the appropriate time and in proper sterile conditions. But Malcolm refused, collected the few belongings he had, and walked out. Pushing all thoughts of infection and further damage to his face out of his mind, he removed the wire himself, using the only instrument he could find – a pair of pliers.

He drove the stolen vehicle on into the dark and bitterly cold night, grateful for the detailed knowledge of every set of lights, crossroads and road bend he would meet. The only difference was the car, depending on what had been simplest to 'acquire' on that particular night. His destination might well have been Bradford, but the journey itself was aimless. It was one of many made 'on the run'; that repeated process of moving from place to place in the hope that it would avoid or at least delay by days, weeks or sometimes months, the inevitable arrest by the police. Malcolm always knew he'd be arrested eventually as he wasn't a good or successful criminal; it was only a matter of time before he'd return to the familiar surroundings of one or other prison to serve yet another sentence. There, the cycle would start again.

He had never been particularly successful in anything but neither did there seem to be an obvious reason for his failure; at least not on the surface. He couldn't claim an especially deprived or disadvantaged upbringing and appeared to receive as many chances as others of his generation and social background. Malcolm's two younger brothers and sister had made the most of their opportunities, working hard, achieving high standards, experiencing success and the full approval of their parents. Parental approval was not something that Malcolm could easily recall. A day rarely went by without him having been the cause of some dispute or upset resulting in punishment of one kind or another. The discovery in later life that he had been conceived out of wedlock, the cause of great social embarrassment, and inconvenience, made him wonder if those thoughts and feelings had simply lingered on into his childhood. There had been little time alone with his parents before the birth of his brothers Raymond and Frank, both of whom arrived before Malcolm's fifth birthday. Learning to share the attentions and affections of his parents with two younger brothers hadn't been easy and then, like so many of his wartime generation, his father was called up to serve in Her Majesty's Forces.

Times were hard during the Second World War and subsequent years, especially for young families like the Worsley household. Money, food and patience were in short supply and anxiety levels ran high. No wife could ever be sure that the father of her children would return from the battle ground alive. Being the eldest child Malcolm frequently took the flack for his younger brothers and absorbed the understandable strains of life upon his young mother. The few memories that remain of that period are almost all negative, centred on a never ending downward spiral of his bad behaviour and punishments. As he grew, so did the expectation that he would misbehave, and Malcolm failed to change what, in hindsight, felt like a united stand against him. One particular incident confirmed these feelings once and for all. It was a day that should have been surrounded with joy and celebration, but remains, one of the most painful and difficult memories of his childhood.

Malcolm was eight at the time and had very little recollection of the father who had set out to fight for his country five years earlier. He recalls the excitement and preparations for the homecoming and most of all, the atmosphere which indicated that something very, very special was going to happen that day.

Malcolm sat on the window sill of their small terrace home. He'd been looking out of the window most of the day wondering when his father would appear at the end of the street. The house was spotless, a special meal had been prepared, the boys were unusually clean and tidy, and his mother dressed in her smartest of clothes. Malcolm wondered what his father would think of him. Would he like him? Would he think he was good; or would he, like the others around him, simply see him as a source of trouble? The emotions were strong, powerful and very mixed. On the one hand he was desperate to see his father, and yet on the other hand, he was fearful that he would be a great disappointment to him.

Petty Officer Robert Worsley came through the door and placed his heavy naval kit bag on the living room floor. There were tears and embraces between the adults as the reunion process began. Malcolm waited for his turn, for the moment which would confirm or allay his fears. Every second seemed a minute, the minutes an eternity, and the kit bag lay in front of him proving too great a temptation for the eight-year-old. After all, he thought to himself, it may even contain a gift for him and his brothers. Surely he had some kind of right to look inside and see what his father had carried home from half way across the world. Leaving his parents to enjoy their reunion he quietly unlaced the top of the kit bag and removed one of the very first items which lay on top. It held no interest for him at all, as he had no idea what it was that he had unpacked. He delved deeper into the bag in search of something both recognisable and more rewarding. It was at this point that Malcolm's father surfaced from his wife's embrace sufficiently to see what his eldest son had done. The unidentified objects, now lightly discarded on the living room floor, were the much valued and precious photographic plates that had travelled hundreds of miles, been carefully packed, and stored to avoid damage or exposure to the light. They now lie in complete ruin, exposed and clearly marked with the fingerprints of a guilty eight-year-old boy. They were the first of many fingerprints that would pronounce Malcolm, guilty.

Without thought or consideration of the possible impact, Bob Worsley shouted, 'You naughty boy. ' They were the first words spoken to his eldest son following a five year absence. On this occasion Malcolm didn't know what his crime had been, but it didn't matter. Those three words answered the question that he had been asking for days; he was clearly not good enough for his father. As the words spun round and round his head something terrifying was happening inside. After five years of waiting his greatest fear had been confirmed – his father didn't like him. He didn't understand, and couldn't control the emotion; something inside hurt and he had to escape from the room. He felt totally responsible for ruining what should have been one of the most important days of their family life. Before anything else could be said Malcolm fled into the scullery and hid underneath the sink clinging onto the lead water pipe for comfort and security.

Aware of some of the trauma that had been caused by his spontaneous outburst Bob Worsley followed his son and tried to coax him out from under the sink. Malcolm refused to be persuaded, despite the tone of mild regret and consolation in his father's voice; it wasn't sufficient to convince the child that he was either forgiven or restored to favour. The increasing combination of anger and frustration at Malcolm's refusal to budge finally resulted in threats of severe punishment – the cycle of which was all too familiar to his daily routine. But, this occasion was more painful than most because it came from the one person from whom he longed to receive affection and warmth, the one he had so wanted to love him and like him. The chances of that ever changing felt remote. Those feelings were simply compounded when, having eventually and reluctantly emerged from under the sink, he was ordered to spend the remainder of the day confined to his bedroom whilst listening to the rest of the family continue the reunion party downstairs. It was a day that marked the conviction, in his own mind, that he was destined to fail.

Malcolm's sister, Joyce, was the much celebrated fourth child born after the war and nearly ten years younger than himself. His pattern of disruptive behaviour had been well established by the time she was old enough to relate to him consequently her memories of him as a child were almost all bad ones. In his desperation to be noticed he regularly displayed senseless, inappropriate, attention seeking behaviour before parents, brothers, sister and peers. The harder he tried the greater the rejection he experienced. He was nearly always the guilty party, and even when, on the rare occasion he wasn't, he became the all too convenient scapegoat for others. Malcolm received the blame and many a beating for his younger brothers. On the surface he always appeared hardened and without feeling whilst on the inside the spirit of a child had been well and truly crushed.

A love of football provided one of the rare enjoyable activities when he could not only burn off the excess energy built up by frustration and anger but experience brief moments of success and acceptance. The only adult whom Malcolm can recall showing him warmth and affection of any kind was his maternal grandfather. The allotments just a few hundred yards from the house became the one place in which he felt safe, secure and wanted. There he was allowed to dig the soil, water the plants, pick the fruits and vegetables and even allowed to make mistakes. His grandfather's correction was always careful and kind, filled with warmth and gentleness. Most of all, he remembers being allowed to climb on his knee where he was held tightly and cuddled, a sure sign that he was loved and accepted. The old man's death when Malcolm was ten years of age left a huge void; an emptiness that he felt he would never ever fill.

It was affection of a very different kind that Malcolm received from one Sunday school teacher. She showed a lot of interest in the twelve-year-old, singling him out from the other boys, and regularly inviting him back to her home for tea. The warmth of her approval, plus the added attraction of egg and chips on a Sunday afternoon, was far more than he could resist. He hadn't banked on having to give anything in return. It wasn't the motherly love that he had hoped for; neither did it bear any resemblance to the affection he had experienced from his grandfather. He was trapped in a vicious cycle of guilt and dependency which felt both right and wrong at the same time.

One particular night when sat with a group of teenage lads, the conversation turned to tales of their early experiences with girls, not least their experimental sexual encounters. The conversation had been jovial and light with the inevitable bragging and exaggerations of stories. As he listened Malcolm realised that none of this was new or experimental to him. His Sunday school teacher had introduced him to such things two years earlier. He suddenly began to experience a growing yet deep inner pain which made him physically sick. The full realisation of what had been happening to him over that two to three year period hit him hard and he became desperate to rid his mind of those memories. He left the group and headed for the nearest pub where he got drunk. The relief was instant but the effects short-lived. It was the beginning of a long road leading to alcoholism and the first occasion on which his parents threw him out of the family home.

By the time Malcolm left school at 15, drinking had become a regular habit. Occasionally he stopped and was allowed back into the family home, but it was rarely for very long. Malcolm had grown all too familiar with failure. Reluctantly he agreed to join his father's building firm as an apprentice and over a period of time acquired a skill that gave him something of lasting value. Those five years offered a degree of stability and security , which all came to a sudden end when at 20, along with many of his peers, he was called up for National Service.

Army life brought drastic changes to Malcolm's lifestyle. It was his first real move away from home and threw him into a regimented work routine that was totally foreign. He responded only because he had to and made few attempts to face the implications of war and the consequences that it might have for him at this stage of his life. But the horrific realities of this time came upon him all too soon - when he was sent into action. Having set sail for the Suez Canal, expecting to join other British forces already engaged in heavy fighting, it came as a shock to be redirected to Malaya. During the course of travel the Suez crisis had come to an end and the troop in which Malcolm served was sent to combat Communist terrorists under the leadership of Chin Peng in Malaya, in what became known as the Malayan War. Malaya in war time was not a pretty experience. Nothing could prepare them for the shocking conditions in which Malcolm and the other young soldiers were expected to live and fight. There could be no pretence; it wasn't a game. The realities of jungle warfare were beyond the wildest of human imaginations; the stench, intense heat, leeches, ringworm and horrific jungle sores were just the beginning. Death, fear, suspicion, terrorism and the sheer hopelessness of many Chinese and Malay's faced him everyday. It became too much to bear; there was no way out.

Malcolm's only relief came in the form of Rum or Anchor and Tiger bitter. Heavy drinking was quite acceptable in the army, almost expected, and supplies readily available. It dulled the senses, took away the pain and distanced the reality of suffering. He welcomed it with open hands and mouth oblivious to the ever increasing quantities he was drinking and the serious long term effects that this would have upon his life. As he had grown accustomed, he lived only for the moment.

The one thing that he valued about army life was that he rarely had to think for himself. He was told when to work, when to sleep, eat and drink! When his demob came in 1959, it was received with a mixture of relief and shock. Yes, he was desperate to leave the horror of Malaya behind but it also meant loosing a whole framework to his life. Suddenly alone and isolated, the only familiar link with the past three years, was the drink. It became a source of comfort and consolation , serving once again to distance the present. Meanwhile he had little desire to face future responsibility in any form.

Yet again circumstances eventually forced Malcolm into action. Josephine his girlfriend since before the war, announced that she was pregnant. Social and family pressures of the day insisted upon marriage, and everything seemed to happen very quickly. At the age of twenty three Malcolm found himself a husband and father to a son, named Alan. Stephen, their second child, arrived only eighteen months later.

Like Malaya, family life wasn't something he had consciously and deliberately chosen; rather it was thrust upon him. Nonetheless, Josephine and his two sons belonged to him; they, along with the drink, became his source of security and comfort. Their home was small and unassuming, a place where he spent very little time, but it was somewhere to belong that was very important to him. He failed miserably as a husband and a father and knew it. When he bothered to work he was capable of earning good money but equally capable of squandering every penny on drink and gambling. Josephine could never rely on Malcolm earning a regular income, and even on special occasions such as Christmas and the boys birthdays he failed to show any concern for their wellbeing or happiness. They regularly went without some of the most basic needs. He could never be trusted and despite promise after promise his every word soon became empty and meaningless to the family.

The urge to drink was greater and stronger than any desire he knew. Every bit of reason deserted him when the longing for alcohol took over. For most of the time drink controlled his life and dictated to him his every waking moment. So it was no surprise to friends, family and neighbours when Josephine decided that she could take no more. He had long since deserted her and the children, only returning home when the money ran out or there was nowhere else to go. At those times he was always drunk. Josephine had tried to help but for the sake of the children she knew that she had to get out of the relationship. With the help and support of her parents who, with good cause, disliked their son-in-law intensely, she took the boys away to stay with an aunt, leaving no forwarding address.

Whilst Malcolm had spent precious little time at home, the absence of both his wife and children was sheer torture to him. He had no-one or nothing to call his own. His parents, brothers and sister had tried on numerous occasions to bail him out of his trouble and give support but each time he abused their trust and took advantage of their expressions of care and concern. On numerous occasions he had tried to assure them that 'this' time would be different, the last time and never again . . . until, of course, the next time. Malcolm had no self control. How it pained them to watch their own flesh and blood wreck both his own and the lives of others.

Desperation drove Malcolm until he found his family in Barnsley, Yorkshire. Penniless as usual he booked into a small hotel nearby knowing full well that he couldn't pay the bill. He wanted a chance to plead with them, to beg them to take him back, making all the same promises that they had heard many times previously. Not surprisingly he failed to convince Josephine but the price of his unpaid hotel bill was costly. It was the first of many prison sentences to come, the beginning of the downward spiral of the next eight years. It was also the seal on his broken marriage. Josephine filed for divorce and finally succeeded in cutting the ties from her estranged and drunken husband. Malcolm could never remember which sentence he was serving when he signed the divorce papers but he knew Josephine and the boys were unlikely to be part of his life again.

From this time onwards Malcolm's life took on the pattern of ever decreasing circles. Individual incidents may well have varied but the overall direction was always the same, round and round, down and down. Prison, release, drink, failure to work, steal in order to eat, months on the run, then finally and inevitably arrest and prison once more. At first Malcolm sincerely believed he could break free and start again. He made several determined efforts with limited success. The pittance of cash and travel warrant given by the Discharged Prisoners Association was barely enough to get him home, never mind provide food and shelter. As for so many released convicts there was never anyone to meet him, and he had no place to go. The routine became a ritual: find rooms, persuade the landlady to give written evidence of the booking, queue at the the Supplementary Benefit Office for rent money, go to the pub and drink the entire week's allowance - leaving nothing with which to pay the rent or eat.

Following one particularly painful 15-month stretch 'inside' Malcolm decided it would be the last. He planned carefully how it would happen. If he could survive a 15-month sentence, he reasoned, surely a self-imposed sentence of one week was easy? Having secured a room for £2 a week he budgeted carefully, bought the bare essentials - a tablet of soap, a razor, some bread and margarine. His T shirt became his towel and there were no other food luxuries. On this occasion luck was on his side and he found a job on a building site working hard, long hours. Each evening he returned to his 'cell' ate his bread and margarine, forbidding himself to go out, determined to survive the sentence.

All went well and he collected what he saw as the first of many pay packets, his first real means to survival for some time. The sense of achievement was great and he felt sure that a celebration called for. But there was only one kind of celebration in Malcolm's books and he took himself off to the pub to enjoy his ration of just one drink. As he stood at the bar the £15 burned fiercely into his thirst for alcohol. He failed to recognise that he was incapable of having just one drink. Gradually as the evening wore on he drank through his only means of survival, a week's wage.

Once on the alcohol trail again he'd do anything to satisfy the burning desire. Breaking into gas and electric meters, stealing any available cash, selling the contents of his rented room, acquiring goods on hire purchase in order to sell them for cash, stealing cheque books, credit cards and the like. How he got the money was unimportant as long as he did it. The single goal in life was to quench that insatiable thirst for alcohol the end of which was always prison.

As time passed he found fewer friends on the outside who were prepared to help and increasing numbers of criminals who wanted his services. Prison was the dustbin of society where one could easily perfect a crime. Malcolm did just that. Word got around as to his usefulness and each release provided him with increased opportunities for more serious crime. In his desire to be accepted and needed he set about the task of proving himself worthy in the eyes of his criminal peers. The petty crimes became more serious, the company more dangerous, and the prison sentences longer.

This particular night, driving from Preston to Bradford, was on the surface typical of many in the last eight years. The only difference lay in the fact that Malcolm knew that he couldn't go on. Perhaps it was the intense pain on this occasion; the broken jaw, dislocated shoulder and sore bruises all reminded him of the events of the last few days. The 'gang' that he had been working with had been excessively violent. The more money 'earned', the greedier he became, most of of the cash being used to buy alcohol and friendship. But on this last job Malcolm had double-crossed them. Having stolen large numbers of television sets from a Yorkshire firm, he was to sell them to contacts in Preston and then share out the money. Instead he kept it all for himself and was now paying bitterly for his failure. Such were 'friends' in the criminal world. Once more he found himself on the run from police, friends and enemies, with nowhere to go.

With the rain beating against the windscreen of the car, it was becoming increasingly difficult to see out or concentrate on driving and so he pulled into a lay by at the side of the road. It was cold and bleak. Behind him the lights of the Salmesbury airfield glared into the darkness. Malcolm lowered his head slowly onto the steering wheel, the pain throbbing throughout his entire body. At first the tears fell slowly and silently but then the floodgates opened. Soon his whole body heaved with the sobbing of a lost and destitute child. He cried out, "God help me – I'm in a mess". It was hardly a prayer as he had no idea to whom or what he might be talking. It was more a desperate cry into the darkness in the hope that someone or something might reply.

Three

A Bradford Vicar

Over the next few days the pain in Malcolm's jaw eased leaving a dull, aching sensation. The hopelessness also lost some of its intensity or at least didn't surface again in quite the same desperate manner as it had done that night. He knew it would always linger inside and unlike his jaw would take more than time to heal. He longed to get out of the vicious circle he was trapped in but had tried many times and failed. Somehow he knew that it wasn't something he could do himself.

Once in Bradford he flitted from place to place, grabbing every offer of accommodation and food as he went. Even within a city he needed to keep on the move, never staying in any one patch for too long for fear that the news of his whereabouts would reach the wrong ears. Some of the members of the crime syndicate he had worked with lived close to Malcolm's girlfriend's house, on one of the many large council estates in the city. News travelled fast, in these parts especially. Though Margaret's was the obvious place for him to stay, it was far too dangerous to be seen there, so his calls were fleeting and often at night.

During one particular visit he managed to persuade her to let him take her four-year-old son Philip with him for a while. He'd be some company and Malcolm knew that it was always easier to secure sympathy, food and money with a child present as people rarely had the heart to turn away a child in need. More importantly the police would be reluctant to stop him with a child sat in the front seat of a car. He knew all the tricks of the trade and was not beyond using even children to further his selfish ends when it suited him.

Having Philip with him worked well for a time until Malcolm started to feel very uneasy, convinced not only that the police knew he was in town but that he was part of the C.I.D. morning briefing. He'd been around for too long, it was time to go – and fast. Normally he would have taken off in whatever vehicle he had in his possession at the time or in one he could acquire quickly, but this time it wasn't quite so easy; Philip was an enormous obstacle. Keeping Philip was no longer practical and might place the child in danger, yet he knew there was far too great a risk involved in returning him to Margaret on the estate, where his pursuers would be waiting for him. There was only one way it could be resolved. In order to ensure Philip's safety he had to find a 'go-between', someone to do the job for him. Rather impulsively he decided on a vicar.

St. John's Church, Great Horton, towered above the surrounding buildings. Built on the hillside, its black Yorkshire stone could be seen for miles around the city. It wasn't the church building itself that Malcolm had noticed especially but the large billboard positioned on the corner of the side street close by, clearly visible to all who travelled up Great Horton Road from the city centre. Passengers on the top deck of buses had a particular close encounter with the large bold letters!

Malcolm had driven passed regularly always automatically reading the many and varied messages; JESUS LIVES, CHRIST DIED FOR YOUR SINS, NEW LIFE IN JESUS. But the one that had stayed with him said, JESUS CHRIST CAN CHANGE YOUR LIFE. Occasionally it would be a longer message with some kind of abbreviated word and numbers following it. His vague recollections from Sunday School days told him that those words came from the Bible. Though he had never given much thought to what he read, what struck him more than anything was that the people responsible for putting up the posters obviously felt they had something important to say to others, the passers-by. Those people he presumed, rightly so, must belong to the church behind. It seemed a good place to start looking for a vicar.

A second smaller notice board outside the church provided Malcolm with the information he needed – the name and address of the vicar. With no time to waste he walked several hundred yards up the road to the vicarage.

Early morning callers were not unusual at the Dracup Road vicarage, especially the needy, homeless and hungry. The recently appointed young vicar was already used to their often exaggerated tales and longed for the wisdom and discernment to distinguish between those genuinely in need and others fabricating some story in the hope of securing sympathy and cash. It wasn't easy, especially when you discover that your vicarage has become one of the many marked houses (literally so) indicating to the community of wandering people whether you're worth a call or not. These folk had quite a network set up in the Bradford district which of course incorporates many vicarages, manses and other charitable institutions.

On this particular morning the Reverend Max Wigley was somewhat puzzled by his visitors. He was thrown slightly by the presence of a small child although that wasn't altogether unusual as 'travelling' families often used their children as emotional weapons to obtain food. But there seemed to be something different about this small, pathetic looking man that didn't quite fit the usual category of such callers. To start with, he was reasonably clean and well dressed - but it was his blunt, bold opening words that made him stand out from others, 'My name is Malcolm Worsley. I'm a criminal with a long record, and I'm on the run from a group of men whom I owe a lot of money. I need your help'.

Max Wigley heard himself inviting them both into the house. Once seated in the study Malcolm hid nothing explaining in detail his criminal dealings and in particular the events of the last few weeks leading up to this meeting. The young vicar sat and listened, quite stunned by the man's blatant honesty, not a quality usually attributed to a criminal. Some minutes passed and as the tale progressed he began to wonder where on earth he fitted into this incredible account, in what possible way he could help such a man. No sooner had the thought crossed his mind than he got his answer. 'I need you to fix up a meeting between me and Margaret so that I can hand Philip over. It's far too dangerous for him to stay with me and far too dangerous for me to go to her. Will you do it, vicar?'

Although Max Wigley had impulsive moments, he was not in the habit of helping criminals out of tight spots so there was nobody more surprised than himself when he realised he'd agreed with little hesitation to act as 'go-between' for Malcolm and Margaret. It seemed a simple task complicated only by the fact that it needed to be done quickly. The two men discussed the details of how, where and when this meeting could take place.

The church itself seemed good neutral ground and so the arrangements were made for a 12 noon meeting. Max agreed to visit Margaret and persuade her to come with him. Malcolm would return with Philip at the appointed hour. Once the child was safely in his mothers arms everyone could go his or her own way. As Max Wigley showed his visitors to the door, he felt confident that he'd made the right decision.

It wasn't until he settled down at his study desk again that the doubts started to surface. Was he aiding a criminal? How could he be sure that his story was true? His head filled with niggling questions and he tried desperately to justify his position. Surely the child was an innocent victim in it all, and he was quite at liberty to offer safety and protection to this young life? As the minutes ticked away, he become less and less sure about what he had committed himself to, but he knew that there was no turning back. Max Wigley respected the trust that had been placed in his hands, also respecting what seemed to him to be a very genuine concern for the welfare of a young child. He had no intention of breaking a promise or abusing the trust he had been given; he'd have to carry out the arrangements as planned.

As the morning went on he became more and more anxious. His restlessness increased, and he couldn't settle to work. By this time he was visualising local newspaper headlines, 'Vicar involved with criminal'. That's all he needed in the early stages of being a vicar of his first church! Still intent on carrying out his bargain, he decided some self protection was in order just in case something went drastically wrong. He picked up the telephone and rang Bradford City Police.

'Is he 5' 8", dark-haired with a pitted complexion?' came the voice down the phone. Max Wigley assured the detective that this description fitted aptly. What followed confirmed his innermost fears and suspicions and he began to wish that he'd accompanied his wife and children to the nursery that morning instead of being available to answer the vicarage door. Warrants were out for the arrest of Malcolm Worsley in several counties, but Bradford Police were especially interested in speaking to him about a series of housebreaking offences. Was he going to be seeing this man again, the detective asked?

Something within him longed to say, 'no'. He hesitated for some seconds before explaining to the police exactly what he had agreed to do and for the child's sake, still intended to do. Thankfully and to his great relief they appreciated the situation and made it quite clear that their only concern was picking up Worsley, not interfering with the arrangements for the child or his mother. Eventually it was agreed that two plain clothes policemen would attend the scene, wait until the handover had taken place and pick up Malcolm for being in possession of a stolen vehicle – a charge which he would undoubtedly be guilty of. It seemed a reasonable compromise and at least Max Wigley felt he'd kept his bargain as far as the child was concerned.

His first move was to track down Margaret on one of the most notorious estates in the city. The presence of a dog collar caused quite a stir in the neighbourhood. It wasn't difficult to find her but standing on the doorstep persuading her both to believe and agree to the plans took slightly longer than he had anticipated. Margaret's mother, with whom she shared a house, objected strongly to the involvement of the young cleric. She had no time for her daughter's involvement with Malcolm Worsley, and it was only concern for young Philip's welfare that stopped her from telephoning the police immediately, a decision she later reversed. After a great deal of persuasion, and much against her mother's wishes, Margaret agreed, for Philip's sake, to accompany him at the appropriate time to the church.

Max Wigley easily spotted the two plain clothes policemen waiting in a stationary unmarked vehicle some ten yards down the side street adjacent to the church. It was seconds before noon. He felt extremely tense, and Margaret was far from conversational. She had no idea of the wider intentions of this meeting, and the vicar sincerely hoped she never would. He planned to allow the couple just minutes to exchange words and most importantly handover Philip. For the child's sake it was important to play things down and get the two of them into his car and away as quickly as he possibly could. The least he could do was take them back home again, even if it was only to convince the disapproving grandmother that he was trustworthy.

Exactly at noon he heard the wheels of a car come suddenly to a halt outside the church gates. He took a deep breath, looked at Margaret and turned to walk towards the car. What confronted him was the worst sight he could have imagined. Just yards in front of them stood a clearly marked police motor patrol car occupied by two uniformed men. Its doors opened and a voice yelled, 'Is 'e 'ere yet, vicar?' Stunned, and extremely angry Max Wigley bellowed back, 'No and he's not likely to be, either, with you sitting there.' After several seconds of speechlessness Margaret suddenly found her voice; convinced that she had been used to trap Malcolm, she expressed her annoyance to the young vicar in no uncertain terms. Coping with his own anger and trying to clear the side street of policemen, poor Max tried to calm an understandably annoyed woman. As if all this wasn't enough, yet another police vehicle suddenly pulled up containing two more plain clothes men.

It was now five past twelve and on the street were no fewer than three police vehicles, six policemen of varying rank, Max Wigley, and a very confused Margaret. At that very moment, right at the bottom of the street Malcolm Worsley came round the corner in his stolen green mini. Without hesitation or consideration of the consequences, Max Wigley ran into the middle of the road waving his arms frantically and shouting, 'Get away! The police are here'. Much to his relief the mini successfully engineered a U-turn, mounting the kerb as it did so, and drove off at great speed up the busy Great Horton Road. Delayed only by the confusion of the situation, two of the police cars followed.

Their chase was unsuccessful as Max Wigley discovered half an hour later when he called in at Odsal Top police station. He hadn't hung around outside the church for explanations or accusations for fear that he might say things he'd later regret. Having safely delivered Margaret to her house he'd had time to calm down and then went in search of the officer responsible for the case. He felt as if it was all a huge fiasco.

It transpired that Margaret's mother had waited until her daughter had left the house, then carried out her threat to ring the police, informing them of the meeting that was about to take place. Unaware of the arrangements that had been made earlier between the vicar and a detective, an officer put out a radio call to all cars in the area to assist in the arrest of Malcolm Worsley. Under normal circumstances the men already assigned to the duty would have responded quickly to the message and assured all concerned that the matter was well in hand. On this occasion, the plain clothes detectives had unfortunately turned off their car radios. Nobody had been more surprised to see the two other patrol cars arrive on the scene!

There was little more that Max Wigley could do. He was relieved to discover that he wasn't under arrest for aiding and abetting a wanted criminal; and after agreeing to notify the police should Worsley reappear, he was free to leave. Whilst driving home he pondered on his days 'work' wondering which part of his theological training was meant to prepare him for such rich experiences. He could hardly believe it had happened but happily filed it into his memory as one of the more unusual incidents in life that he could always recount to his grandchildren in years to come.

Having put the incident behind him Max turned off the main road into the small side street where his vicarage stood. His mind had already begun to focus on the church council meeting planned for that evening … until the sight of a green mini parked alongside the vicarage garden wall gave him a shock. Immediately fearful for his wife and children inside the house, he leapt out of the car and through the front door. Within seconds the door bell rang. Malcolm pushed his way into the house, this time alone, having dumped Philip elsewhere. The same small, pathetic but desperate-looking man pleaded for help. This time he had little success; Max made it clear that the only grounds for help were if Malcolm agreed to give himself up. Much discussion and persuasion took place until yet another meeting was arranged, at the vicarage. Malcolm was to deliver both Philip and himself into the hands of the police, where appropriate action would be taken for both. Malcolm left and Max informed the police.

Not surprisingly, Malcolm failed to keep the appointment.

Four

The Risley Experience

'City police, here vicar. We have one of your flock with us and he's asking to see you.'

It was Malcolm, finally under arrest and claiming his right to one phone call. That call wasn't, as is usual, to a solicitor, but to the vicar who had helped him escape from the police two weeks earlier. The sight of Max Wigley standing in the middle of the road waving him away from six policemen had stuck firmly in his mind. Many times since that incident he had wondered exactly what kind of vicar this man was, even if the impact hadn't been sufficient to cause him to return to the vicarage and give himself up as arranged.

It was with mixed emotions that Max Wigley drove to the city police cells. Part of him was thrilled that Malcolm had wanted to see him, but the other part was suspicious of the man's motives, and he could not help wondering if he was the next in line to be conned by this able criminal. By now he had done his homework and learned something about him from both social and probation services. Everyone he spoke to had issued the same warnings; 'Have nothing to do with him. He's a thoroughly bad person and has hardly been out of prison in 10 years.' Seemingly there were no limits to his wicked activities, and everyone who had tried to help had been either robbed or conned in the process. It seemed that the 'professionals' had well and truly dumped Malcolm Worsley upon the rubbish heap of society and perhaps, thought Max Wigley, with real cause; so he would tread cautiously.

Clutching a recently published modern translation of the New Testament (the Good News Bible), he approached the town hall. He didn't understand the complexities of a criminal mind or of the criminal world, but he did know that the only hope for Malcolm was to be found in the pages of this paperback book. He felt inadequate but was determined to explain something of the new life that could be found in God.

Once Max was inside the cell Malcolm tried fervently to explain the reason why he had failed to turn up at the vicarage that day. It was a pathetic sight and Max, on this occasion, needed little wisdom to see through the superficial lies and excuses. It was no surprise to learn that for the last two weeks Malcolm had simply drifted from place to place, from pub to pub, acquiring cash one way or another as he went.

Max sat quietly as Malcolm told of his inner struggle, the longing to be arrested and yet lacking the courage to walk into the police station and give himself up. The end had finally come that lunch time when two off duty police officers had walked into the Queensbury pub where he was mulling over a pint of bitter. He recognised them immediately and knew also that, given the opportunity, they too would recognise him. It seemed the time to end his misery and approaching them at the bar he had announced without emotion, 'I'm Malcolm Worsley, wanted by the police both here and in Preston. Please take me in.' This was no great achievement in Malcolm's eyes as all he could think of at the time was cutting himself off from the alcohol he so desperately craved and thought he needed. Now, just hours later, he regretted the decision. Sitting locked up in the city cells he felt quite frantic and the Bradford vicar seemed his only hope.

The tale was followed by all manner of pleas for help and promises of change. Max listened patiently, wanting to believe what he was now hearing. No more crime, no more alcohol, a change of heart, direction, a change of life. How many times had he heard similar determined cries of the heart from folk with far fewer complications in life than Malcolm? He thought how comparatively simple his church members pastoral problems were and vowed never to complain again about listening to them. Sitting here looking at the bedraggled figure before him he felt momentarily hard and cynical, even unbelieving.

Opening up the New Testament at St John's gospel, chapter 3, he read aloud the story of Nicodemus. Looking Malcolm straight in the eyes he said, 'Malcolm you must be born again. It is the only way your life and personality can be changed. Jesus is the only person who can do it. Take this book and read it, for in it you will find your new life, new direction and hope for the future.'

It meant little to Malcolm. He looked as confused as Nicodemus had been when Jesus first spoke those words to him. Malcolm wanted concrete facts and evidence, something that he could hang on to. Max continued to read parts of the New Testament this time from Matthew's gospel: 'I tell you not to be worried about the food and drink you need in order to stay alive, or about clothes for your body ... Instead, be concerned above everything else with the Kingdom of God and with what He requires of you, and He will provide you with all these other things.'

Now that he could understand–but whether he could believe it was another matter. Laughing, he challenged Max, 'What? God provide me with food, drink and clothes? You've got to be kidding me vicar ! Will he provide me with a house too? No God can do that sort of thing!'

The vicar could see the seeming absurdity of it all from Malcolm's viewpoint, yet he knew it was the truth. God could change this man's life, set him upon a new track and provide him with more than he should ever need or desire. But it was his choice, his decision, and nobody could do it for him.

Before leaving he slipped an address card into the cover of the New Testament and handed it to Malcolm. He told him that he would pray for him every day, asking God to bring him to repentance and faith in Jesus. For the third time in two weeks Max Wigley said goodbye without knowing if he'd ever see or hear from this man again.

It wasn't difficult to get a signed statement from a man like Malcolm. Two detectives escorted him across the Pennines back to Preston, where the earlier police warrant had been put out for his arrest. En route they stopped at a moorside pub and filled him with enough alcohol until he signed their prepared statement. At that stage of alcohol withdrawal he would have signed anything for a drink.

Once in Preston the routine was all too familiar. He occupied a station cell until called by the magistrate, who refused bail and ordered him to Risley Remand Centre. There was never any question of bail for Malcolm; he knew that no one was prepared to risk money for his sake.

Risley, or 'Grisley Risley' as the inmates called it, was a purpose-built, top-security prison where criminals of every description came and went, each awaiting their court appearance and sentence. It was a grey, concrete, soulless building and emotions ran high as anxious first time petty offenders lived nervously alongside hardened and seasoned criminals.

Malcolm's memories of these short-term confinements in this and other prisons were not good. One vivid and particularly painful occasion was back in 1960 in Walton, Liverpool – the last hanging of a British criminal – an occasion that went down in history. It wasn't the kind of experience that he ever wanted to remember, yet it was one that he could never forget.

Such executions always took place in the morning, and no man was allowed out of his cell on that day. Prison officers walked around under a black cloud of silence that brought gloom and doom to the whole building, until the appointed hour when the hanging took place. Then slowly and gradually each man would take his metal drinking mug and strike up a slow rhythm of banging against his cell door. This protest death chant of mugs gathered more and more participants until the whole building vibrated with the dirge of death. Sometimes it continued for hours, no man daring not to join in for fear of his fellow prisoners. The heaviness remained throughout the long hours of the day, dying away only in the darkness of the night.

Malcolm knew that this was one experience that he would never have to live through again, for which he was deeply grateful. But Risley he still did have to face, plus his court hearing and the inevitable sentence. Only one thing was different on this occasion; the New Testament that went with him.

He started by reading the gospels, some parts of which he remembered from his days at Sunday school as a child. But for Malcolm by far the most interesting and fascinating section of the New Testament was the book of the Acts of the Apostles. He read and reread it tirelessly, not just once but sometimes six or seven times a day, every day of the week. There was something about the life of St Paul that captivated him. Saul (later called Paul) was responsible for keeping the Christians in order, suppressing their new found faith and preventing them from preaching and teaching about Jesus Christ. He regularly ordered men and women from their homes into prison and stood by watching the stoning of Stephen, the first Christian martyr. Yet this same man, only months later, was himself imprisoned for speaking about the same faith as those whom he had persecuted. Malcolm was intrigued. What had brought about such a drastic change in this man's life, and was it possible that his own life might be changed to the same degree? He read on in search of the answer to his questions. Reading the Bible came a lot easier than praying. Gripped though he was by the life and journeys of St Paul, he didn't always know in his own mind who or what God was. Despite all he was reading and wanting to believe there were still moments when he even doubted the existence of a God. He remembered how Max Wigley had told him to pray, to speak to God and ask His forgiveness, but he struggled desperately, wanting something or someone to focus his prayers on. Out of sheer desperation and determination he looked up at the light bulb and spoke aloud, ' Dear God, Max Wigley says if I ask, you will help. I don't know who or what you are so I'm speaking to the light bulb. I don't know if this will work but I'm going to try. I'm going to keep on reading this book and I promise to keep looking for the answers. I've nothing to lose.'

Day after day the Bible reading continued and the same prayer was repeated always directed towards the light bulb. By now Malcolm was mapping out the missionary journeys of St Paul drawing his information not only from the book of Acts but from all of Paul's letters to the early churches. He was not satisfied until every detail fell into place.

It was while he was searching for an answer to what he thought was an inconsistent teaching in the New Testament that, for the first time, he sensed the living presence of God in his cell. He spoke to God. 'Come on, God, what does this mean? I don't understand, surely there is something amiss here? Please show me what I need to know.' There was no immediate answer to his question, no voice from heaven, yet the silence had been broken. At that precise moment God had broken through the roof, through the light bulb and was with him in the cell. Malcolm knew that he had just spoken to a person. The question drifted into insignificance, for what he was experiencing was far greater and more important than any question. God was there. God was *there*. The words went round and round inside him. He couldn't see him or touch him but there was no doubt that He was there. He hardly dare move for fear that this visitor might go away. It was overwhelming. Finally he managed to sit on the edge of his bed, bowed his head and spoke; 'Lord God, I know you're real, here right now. Please, please, let Jesus help me just as He did Paul'. It was only the beginning. Praying, he discovered, brought him into the presence of God in a way he had never experienced before. He could talk to him just as if he were a person standing in the same room. And the conversations became two-way. But God didn't use human words. His presence spoke of power, holiness and a purity that was quite foreign to Malcolm. He sat for long periods of time feeding on the stillness and learning to sense something of the vast and awesome nature of this God.

As he sat in the silence images came into his mind; pictures of his past and in particular of the crimes he had committed. They were painful reminders of the criminal mind and deeds that had dominated the last ten years. Watching them flash past his minds eye, in the presence of God, was agonising.

Every picture varied, but rarely was there a time when they didn't appear. One was especially painful. It took him back to a day he had burgled a small terrace house in broad daylight. Having successfully broken into a gas meter and confident that the way was clear, he made a swift exit through the rear garden of the house. He had not seen the small fair-haired girl standing behind the garden wall. Therefore he almost ran into her when pulling open the back gate. For a brief moment he hesitated, unsure of what to say or do. There were only the two of them in the back alley and he needed to move quickly so he resorted to shouting down at the child in a loud threatening voice. He was some yards away before he dare turn round to see the effects of his booming words and it was this picture that had surfaced in his minds eye now. A petrified three-year-old stood paralysed by fear, eyes filled with tears that were about to flood her pale cheeks. She was lifting a finger to the corner of an eye and taking a deep breath ready to scream.

The image haunted Malcolm and wouldn't leave him until he looked the child in the eye and faced up to the pain that he had put her through. Only when he was full of disgust and shame for his action did the picture stop coming. It was the start of a long process that made him face up to the realities of all he had done.

Day after day he begged God to take away the horrendous pictures of himself that were now flooding his mind day and night. He tried to stop praying in the hope that they would disappear, but it was no good. 'God I'm sorry', he repeated over and over again, desperate to be forgiven. But he could find no peace. All God seemed to be saying was, 'No you're not, Malcolm. You don't know what being sorry is. Look and remember all you have done. You did those things, Malcolm. You're guilty of all that.' Malcolm retorted, 'I am sorry, really sorry, I didn't mean to do them.' The more he cried, the more God showed him his wretchedness; every single sin of his life came to the surface and he was forced to look at them all. The torture was unbearable, the pain unrelenting, and he could stand it no longer. He felt there was no future. Life couldn't go on in this state.

By now he was drifting around in a state of semi-consciousness, not having slept for several weeks. Tears streamed permanently from his eyes, and he spent hours of the day curled up under his bunk in an attempt to hide from himself and God. He'd always prayed seated or curled in a tight ball on his bed. For some reason this particular night he sensed God telling him to get on his knees. Already totally humiliated and unable to face himself, he considered this final act of submission impossible. He had nothing else to say or do before God. How could He ask him to go on his knees in that state? The answer was a definite 'No', but the niggling request returned throughout the night as he tossed and turned in his bunk. As the early hours of the morning approached, in desperation, to end the torture inside Malcolm fell onto his knees at the side of his bunk and prayed what he was sure would be his last prayer; 'OK God, you win. I am the worst person who ever lived. I know that I'll never get into your kingdom, I'm too bad. I deserve nothing. I'm worse than Paul. I admit it, so now leave me alone. Let me get on with my life, just leave me alone.'

Returning to his bunk feeling confident that he'd finally got God out of his system, Malcolm slept longer and more deeply than he had done in weeks. No more scenes from the past flashing through his mind or recurring nightmares. No tossing and turning in his bunk. It was pure, blissful, childlike sleep. The battle was over and God had won.

A new day dawned and a new man awoke. Aware that he had slept for the first time in weeks he stood up a little bemused, struggling to recall the events of the night. Everything had changed; the cell, the air that he breathed, his body – absolutely everything about him and around him was different. He took a deep breath, his chest expanding inches further than it had ever done before. He felt lighter and warm; the air had a freshness and vitality in it that he'd never previously known. Inside he felt clean and pink, new and special. Like a mother examining a new born baby, he stared at his arms and legs and counted the fingers on his hands. The sky looked blue; the sun blazed through the tiny window.

It was as if a surgeon had taken a scalpel and removed the past, once and for all. An enormous weight had been lifted from his shoulders and dumped somewhere along the Damascus Road. His torture had ended in that final admission and submission to God. Now he understood what had happened to St Paul all those years ago and the same thing had happened to him. It was all God's doing, none of his own. The past had been wiped out. He was forgiven, and he knew he had a place in heaven along with his hero Paul. It was indescribable.

As he stood locked in his cell, Malcolm Worsley realised that this was a freedom far greater than he had ever experienced before. He had met with a God of new beginnings, of new birth and hope. His searching had come to an end and yet somehow he knew that his new life had only just begun.

Five

Letters From Prison

The Risley experience had been powerful and unforgettable. Even Malcolm struggled to believe the change in himself. For the first time in years he wanted to laugh out loud and run around like a young child let loose in a garden on a sunny day. The sunshine came from within and shone out through his eyes and smile; his garden was the cell, corridors and canteen. It left prison officers and cell mates puzzled but undisturbed. They were quite sure that whatever experience he had had, religious or otherwise, it would not have any lasting effect. Prison life succeeded in squashing anything that might be remotely good or positive.

Malcolm knew it would take time to prove just how different he was. So far it had just been an experience that even he hadn't fully grasped. Actually explaining it to others seemed impossible. He simply felt different and knew that he was no longer carrying around a lifetime's guilt. Couldn't others see it? How was he meant to put that sense of relief and freedom into words? They ridiculed him tirelessly at first, but their scorn was like water off a duck's back. Nobody was going to take away this wonderful experience; as far as Malcolm was concerned, it was there to stay.

Exactly how he was going to walk those first few steps at the start of his new life he didn't know. He felt like a newborn baby. There was no midwife or parent to spoon or bottle feed him; no one to catch him when he fell or bathe the cuts and bruises when he was hurting. But Malcolm had every intention of trying with or without help. The last few weeks (and years!) had been hell, and now he had had a taste of heaven and no one was going to take it from him.

There was only one person in the world to whom Malcolm felt able to turn: Max Wigley. He was his only friend, the only non-criminal that he knew. Everybody else had long since given up on him and were unlikely to believe any further tales or explanations about his latest good intentions. But Malcolm knew he had to earn his right to speak, to convince this vicar that he was sincere in his search for faith. He tried very hard to impress upon him the fact that he was a genuine seeker. The first of many letters read:

Dear Mr Wigley
You may be surprised to know that I have made a point of reading the New Testament you gave me for at least an hour a day. The gospels although similar in their accounts of Christ's life I found very interesting and enjoyable. The Acts of the Apostles was probably to me the more stimulating. It has been these last three days, when I have been reading Paul's letter to the Romans and Corinthians, that I have found it rather heavy going. I am going to try and contact the chaplain here to see if he has a booklet helping people to understand these letters more clearly. In the meantime I am rereading St. Luke.

You mentioned in your letter that you would try and get someone to come and see me. If you could arrange this, I would be most grateful. There is no limit to the amount of visits we have and they are daily (except Sundays) between 1.30pm and 4pm.

Freedom is nothing until you lose it. A lot of people don't even appreciate what freedom is, myself included. I honestly and sincerely pray to God that there will be a solution to my way of life. I am most grateful for your encouragement so far and if I can mention part of St. Matthew's gospel, it proves to me that people are prepared to help. The passage I have in mind is Chapter 25 verses 31-46. These verses show that God has no time for hypocrisy and only those who carry on their lives in a true manner are acceptable in God's eyes.

I reread St John's gospel again as you said, chapter 3 was a great help. Tonight I will be reading the letter from James. I hope to hear from you soon.

All the best
Yours sincerely, Malcolm

Malcolm wrote as often as his prison allowance allowed him to buy stamps. It was always once, sometimes twice or even three times a week. The replies were not as frequent as he would have liked and at the early stages of their correspondence Max expressed great caution in his writing. Despite his daily prayers for Malcolm, he still had to be sure that he wasn't being taken for a ride. Early on in their relationship he wrote;

Dear Malcolm
Thank you for your letters. By now you should have received my letter, plus stamps and pen.

I was thrilled to bits that you had read the New Testament I gave you. As you say, the books of the Romans and Corinthians are heavy going unless you have something to help you understand the background to the books. But press on and perhaps you are right to reread Luke's gospel as such an understanding of Jesus and His ministry is essential to finding Him as your own Saviour and Lord.

There is only one solution to your way of life as it is, and that is Jesus Christ. There is no other way for a person to be changed, only in the power of God. From the probation service and other people I know your background very well now, Malcolm. I want to help by writing to you but don't try to con me; I'm the wrong sort. If you sincerely want help to find a new way of life, then I will help you by pointing you to Christ. But if I find that you are conning me I'm afraid we will part company.

I have found that you have lied to me about several matters or perhaps not told me the whole truth with the intent of deceiving. You have a reputation to live down, and it is only God who can help you to do it. Your letters themselves are deep and interesting and it is obvious that you are interested in the subject of the Lord Jesus. It is not a matter of me trusting you but of you proving to me that you can be trusted. I certainly want to give you every opportunity. I continue to pray for you daily that you might find new life in Christ and the strength and power to begin again.

Best regards, Max Wigley

Max had never been so involved with helping a criminal before. He was anxious to do and say the right things but at the same time realised that he was perhaps naive and inexperienced in relating to such people. Friends had been keen to offer him all sorts of advice, much of which had been based on their own negative experiences. It would have been easier to dismiss Malcolm as 'not his problem', but something within spurred him on in his writing. By now members of his congregation had joined him in praying daily for this convict.

He was very careful at first to resist the temptation to respond to Malcolm's continual pleading to visit him in Risley. The letters and requests came thick and fast and although the distance was not too great he decided to restrict his contact to letters. It seemed in the circumstances the best way to test this man's sincerity.

Over the weeks Malcolm's letters changed from constant attempts to prove himself to more subdued reflection on his circumstances and future. This was the first real indication to Max that he was facing the realities of his situation and serious about living a Christian life. It wasn't too long before he faced his first real test. His court hearing date was fast approaching, and he was dreading its outcome. He reflected upon his position and the likely sentence in a letter to Max;

Dear Mr Wigley

It is not long until I appear in court. I wish I could think that some alternative to plain prison would be given to me but I think it most unlikely. Turning everyone against me as I have done over the last couple of months has really sealed my coffin. To get the courts to offer to help you to reform needs support, and I have nobody at the moment. Over the past few weeks I have been wondering what I could say in way of mitigation to the recorder when I appear before him. So many thoughts and ideas have passed through my mind, but in the end, it all boils down to one thing. I am guilty and nothing I nor anyone else can say can alter the fact. All I hope for is that the recorder will find the answer to me, somewhere in the reports he will have on me.

At least prison will give me time to study my Bible and perhaps I can use it to shield against 'nick' talk. I was beginning to think that the Church as a whole was just like the prison church, but since you gave me the Bible to read I can see that it isn't. I'd have never thought to look for God in this place if I hadn't come to the vicarage that day about ten weeks ago now.

Best wishes, Malcolm.

Considering the circumstances Malcolm thought it unlikely that he would receive anything less than a two-and-a-half to three-year sentence for his crime, so the news of twenty-one months felt to him a miracle. It was the chance he needed to stop and take stock of all that had happened in the previous few months; the chance to set himself realistic targets and hit them. As much as he would have loved to have walked free from the courts that day he knew he had a price to pay for his crime and needed time to work at his new found faith before being let loose into the world again. Soon he started his sentence in Liverpool jail.

As well as the help given by Max Wigley in his letters, books became a most valuable source of encouragement for him in these first few stages of growth. The prison library was extremely limited but did provide a little stimulation for this inquiring mind. Study had never been his favourite pastime; in fact he couldn't remember the last time he had actually read a book –

perhaps while still at school nearly fifteen years ago. But now he was searching out all the reading matter that he could find to keep this renewed mind alive.

In the prison library, mixed in with thrillers and western stories, Malcolm found various translations of the Bible which he delighted in comparing with each other. He sat daily with three or four versions open at the same passage comparing the words and phrases. Numerous questions surfaced in his mind and were automatically directed at Max, whose time was increasingly spent ploughing through theological texts in an attempt to produce the answers. The questions seemed endless.

How many modern translations were there, and how did they differ from each other? Was it wise to have so many different 'interpretations' of the same story? Was Luke one of Paul's converts, and if so why was it that he was able to write so accurately of Jesus' life and teachings, since Paul was converted after the death of Christ? Could it be that Mark and Luke had met and discussed their writings? What about the various source documents? Why was it that the Old Testament seemed complicated?

Malcolm's insatiable thirst for learning had replaced a thirst for alcohol. He had moved from self destruction to the rebuilding of his body, mind and spirit. Contact with prison chaplains from the various denominations (always failing to see the need for such divisions) provided further channels for study. On arriving at Liverpool he enrolled on his first Bible study course and signed up for the weekly study class with a few other prisoners. His understanding and confidence grew fast until, instead of asking numerous questions in his letters to Max, they became an account of all that he had learned that week. And his sense of fun and humour emerged too:

Dear Mr Wigley

I have been waiting all week to be able to buy a stamp so that I can write to you and apologise for not spotting your deliberate mistake sooner. As you will know from my last two letters I spent a great deal of my time during my last week at Risley studying the Resurrection, and it was not until I got here that I continued again with Paul. By the way if your reference of Acts 4.4 is not a deliberate mistake might I suggest 500 lines? As to whether Luke was ever in Colossae I would not like to say, but I do know that Paul never went there, even though he must have been quite near on a number of occasions.

The church at Colossae was probably started by Epaphroditus, who was later imprisoned in Rome with Paul. Paul's only contact with the church there was through his letter to them from Rome, probably in prison in 62 AD. I don't know whether you are looking for some indication from me that I am indeed studying the Gospels and Epistles.

After all, isn't Paul proof of the living church? A persecutor turned preacher. I cannot get away from the power and strength behind his preaching. What a wonderful experience it must have been that gave him the courage to overcome several beatings, whippings, a stoning, shipwrecks and imprisonment. The sufferings of the early apostles is proof beyond doubt that it was something more than mortal they were fighting for.

I have found a couple of verses which I read every day. They are in Paul's letter to the Ephesians chapter 4 v.28-32, beginning 'He who has been stealing must steal no longer, but must work, doing something useful with his own hands ...' I have also been trying to read a book by Father Herbert on the Christian Community but all it has taught me so far is that modern church politics is best left alone. There are so many divisions in the Christian church that some are almost like different religions.

Best wishes, Malcolm.

The study continued intensively, encouraged by Max's regular letters and by this time an occasional visit from Bradford. These visits meant a great deal to Malcolm, more than he could ever express in words. He had a friend who wasn't a criminal, someone that he could trust and rely upon for support and encouragement. He kept every letter received from Max reading and re-reading them daily in his cell. Along with his Bible they were fast becoming his life line, without which he knew he would sink.

Dear Malcolm

Thank you for your last two letters. I'm sorry I put the wrong text when referring to Luke knowing Paul; it should have been Colossians 4:4 and not Acts 4:4. I assure you that it wasn't a deliberate mistake. I'm thrilled you are learning so quickly about your scriptures. Of course, head knowledge is important but heart knowledge is most important. We can know all about theology without knowing Christ as a living person in our lives.

Don't worry, Malcolm, I'm not trying to trip you up. It's obvious from your letters that you are really studying the scriptures and that you have great potential in the academic sense. If you went to night school and got stuck in you would very soon find yourself with some good qualifications. I'm glad to hear that you're getting stuck into the Bible study class. I haven't read the book you mentioned but it's obviously very interesting.

Anyway, I'd better close Malcolm. Please keep writing. Although I cannot write as frequently as you, I will endeavour to answer your letters when I can. I continue to remember you in prayer and that you might find Christ as a person who can forgive your past, give you power to live the life you want now and give you certainty in a world that has none.
With best wishes, Max.

The new life that Malcolm had found in Christ was changing everything. He fought daily to bring his body, mind and spirit under the influence and control of God's Holy Spirit, yet he was never under any illusion as to the real opposition he faced. His life was modelled on that of his hero St Paul. If Paul could endure such hardships in the power of God, so could Malcolm, or at least he was determined to try. The one thing they both had in common was their experience of prison.

Grateful though he was for the time and opportunity for learning, he knew even at this early stage of his stay in prison that the ultimate test would come at the end of his sentence. He never stopped wondering if his faith would be strong enough when that time came and openly expressed his fears and concerns about this:

Dear Max

Sometimes I feel that imprisonment isn't hard on a person. It deprives him of his liberty, but that's all. The punishment part of a sentence doesn't start until you are RELEASED! This is when you have to face society with £4 in your pocket and a blank insurance card. On top of this, you have a record (for the rest of your life), and therefore your choice of jobs is limited. I'm not saying that it is impossible to live down a past, because I would be lying; but it is made difficult by the red tape that ties together our legal and aftercare system. I think that's enough backbiting for one letter and anyway I'm sure that you are aware of these 'practical' problems.

Spiritual problems are another matter, and particularly your reference to a heart experience with Jesus Christ. At the time of writing I am fully aware that Jesus Christ lives in the world today and can forgive us our sins. I want to be honest with you, Max, and at the same time be honest with myself. I would like to believe here and now that I will come out of prison a Godfearing Christian, and I pray to our Lord Jesus Christ every night that this will happen. But locked away in here it is quite easy to lose all perspective of reality. As you know we live behind an eighteen foot wall in a closed community and therefore there are no social temptations. Was it Karl Marx who said, 'religion is the opiate of the masses'? This is how it appears to work in here from what I've been told. You are not faced with the temptations of a modern society and therefore there is little scope for sinning. In a situation like this it is quite easy to kid ourselves that we have found Christ and that religion is the answer. Of course it is the answer and the only answer, but will this environmental acceptance of Christ stay with us when we are released? Or will it, like an opiate, wear off?

I have thought a lot about this and I feel I would be cheating on you if I did not mention it. I feel 99.999% sure that the feeling I have in my heart for Christ is a lasting one. I know what it means to love, to care for people and to understand the glorious sacrifice that Christ made for us. I feel stronger and stronger every day that Christ can make something of me. I feel a lot happier now than I have in a long time and really when you think about it I have no 'practical' reason to be.

By the way, the second letter of Paul's to the Corinthians—was the last chapter written by Paul? The rest of the letter although jerky in parts is a very moving and sincere epistle, but the last chapter seems completely out of context. I'd be grateful for your comments. Don't neglect the important business to write to me.

With best wishes through Christ, Malcolm.

Max was hopeful that Malcolm would remain in Liverpool for the rest of his sentence as he had reason to visit the city regularly and so could call at the prison. He also knew a number of clergymen in the area who would do the same. But it wasn't to be. By the middle of January 1971 Malcolm had been sent to Haverigg in Cumbria to serve the remaining ten months at this open prison. It was isolated, bleak, and very difficult to reach. Max thought it unlikely that he would ever find the opportunity to travel so far and so decided that, apart from their written correspondence, he had to find someone else to encourage and visit Malcolm during these critical months. Will Barker, a Scripture Union worker, became that person.

Six

Haverigg

Will Barker had considerable experience working with offenders, especially youngsters who had been sent to approved schools and borstals. Over the years he had grown to understand something of the problems faced by these young people, especially the struggle they encountered trying to earn a place back in society after a period of time inside institutions of this kind. Occasionally his work took him into prisons where the problems were even greater, intensified by repeated failure and rejection by society. Will had a real burden for these boys and men and longed for them to find a new beginning with God in the world at large. His life was dedicated to that task.

The invitation from Max Wigley to go to Haverigg to visit Malcolm delighted him. There was no greater joy to him than nurturing a new Christian in the faith, knowing the opposition that he would find inside prison. Will was determined to do all that he could to encourage this man and so their first meeting was arranged very soon after Malcolm's arrival.

'Will', Malcolm said, 'Can I tell you how I met Jesus?' For the next fifty minutes he relayed his story to the transfixed Will Barker, who neither spoke nor moved as he listened to the tale. Never before had he met anyone quite so free and yet confined within the perimeters of prison walls. In all his years of ministry amongst offenders he had never encountered such a powerful testimony as this. He saw quite clearly the impact of God upon this man's life and began to sense the privilege he now had in helping him on this journey of faith. As Will drove away from Haverigg later that day he wondered who had benefited most from the visit, himself or Malcolm? It was the first of many and the foundation of what was to become a close, affectionate relationship.

There was little doubt that Malcolm would need Will's support in the days ahead despite his bubbly enthusiasm at the start. Haverigg brought him a lot of 'stick' from cell mates and fellow prisoners. He wasn't surprised as it was common practice for newcomers to be 'put through the mill', and he knew the routine well. But now, as a Christian, he expected it to be far worse - and he was right. He braced himself, willing to suffer for the sake of Jesus Christ and eager at all times to follow the example of his hero St Paul. His only guideline was the New Testament, and from what he had read he understood that every Christian should expect persecution of some kind; therefore he should take his in a spirit of rejoicing, glad he was considered worthy of such suffering.

These experiences so early on in his Christian life served to strengthen his faith and make him determined to keep going, whatever the cost. As the weeks went by his desire to speak about what God had done for him increased. He took every opportunity he could.

'The prison', he wrote to Max, 'is run on the basis of an army camp, inside a wire enclosure. Mountains and hills swell up around us, a bleak but beautiful sight. Inside the wire we live fairly well. We have a choice at meal times and the beds are clean and comfortable. I told the welfare officer that I have put all my problems in God's hands. He is a Jehovah Witness, so I thought it wise not to mention that I am a dedicated blood donor!'

A sense of humour was so important on the 'inside' and Malcolm tried hard to show his fellow prisoners that life under lock and key needn't be unbearable. Of course they were not convinced that the newcomer had anything of value to offer them and proceeded to amuse themselves at his expense. He became the object of name-calling, ridicule and pranks, especially the ones that risked his getting into trouble with prison officers. Malcolm remained philosophical and unwavering in his faith knowing that only time and continued good example would silence their laughter. As he saw it, many wanted to talk about God but were simply too embarrassed to do so. He explained to Max:

There is an odd lad who continues to have a go at me, but really I don't mind, and I can turn it to my advantage. They usually greet me with "Good morning vicar", cross themselves, and tell me that this 'God jazz' is no good, and that it is the brainchild of a con man. As I see it, with no encouragement from me they are speaking about God, and I want them to talk more about Him. This only serves to remind me that my every minute and action should be worthy of Him who gave up His life for me. Paul was obviously influenced by the tremendous faith of Stephen, who forgave all his persecutors in his final prayer. I too must withstand this persecution, in love for these men.

The men became Malcolm's priority, his first mission field as an evangelist. He felt deep compassion for them all, knowing full well the gap between being a criminal and a Christian, and longing for them to experience the love and forgiveness he had found in Christ, the new life that he was now living. As time went on, they couldn't fail to notice the difference in him; and despite their provoking and abuse many asked Malcolm to tell them how he found God. There seemed hardly a day when he didn't have an audience of one kind or another. He took these opportunities seriously working out how he could clearly explain what had happened to him and encourage others to seek the same thing. He shared many of these times with Max:

> I tried to tell Joe, Pete, Steve, Tony, Ray and Bob how I came to know God and was surprised at how difficult I found it to explain. Thinking about it afterwards I decided it all comes down to two things. Firstly we have to WANT God to help us; and secondly we have to BELIEVE that God can help us. I know I experienced difficulty praying to God because I did not know Him. But I asked Jesus to help me over this even though I didn't know him at the time. It is surprising that if we pray to God and tell Him that , even though we don't know what He is or where He is – He will help us.

Malcolm had his work cut out answering all the questions fired at him by the men. Some were sincere, genuine searching questions, and others thrown out to trick and trip him. 'Why', one man asked , 'was my father maimed in a work accident, crippled and continually in pain for life?' Another wanted to know why, if Jesus could still a stormy sea, did God allow church steeples to be struck by lightning? How Malcolm struggled with convincing the Jewish prisoners of the Messiahship of Christ. Even his personal exposition of the book of Hebrews and an outline of Old Testament prophecy didn't appear to help.

All of his free time was now centred on bringing these men to a knowledge and experience of Christ. It was a slow process but in time he began to see the fruits of his labour. Informal discussions in the cells became organised groups and Bible studies, and Malcolm's companions boosted the numbers at every denominational service in the prison. It was unimportant to him as to how people worshipped, as long as the message of Jesus was preached. There were however moments of great frustration when, in his eyes, the services failed to communicate anything of lasting value to the convicts. In desperation one day he poured out his woes to Max:

> I have been wondering again this past week or two whether there is something wrong with my outlook on Christianity. I believe that we should preach Jesus by keeping our faith simple. Christ is the church and the doorway to eternal life. I believe that the Holy Spirit is a MUST in all our services here. I firmly believe that if we hand over the meeting to Him and have faith He will work amongst us. Then who can doubt His influence? I prayed really hard for the numbers to increase, and through the power of the Holy Spirit working in and among us the numbers rose. Our meetings have gone well when we have spoken of the new

life offered through Christ Jesus, but once again this week the numbers are down. Why? The chaplain has gone all 'choral' again. Why, in the name of all I believe in will he not allow the Holy Spirit to use all of us to bring Christ into these services. Hymns are very nice and I enjoy singing but can Catholics, Pentecostals and Methodists sing to Anglican chants?

Honestly Max I begin to wonder whether I've got the message back to front. I dearly love our Lord, and if I sound pious it is only because I really and truly do believe in Jesus Christ the Saviour of Mankind. I reach boiling point sometimes when lads come up to me and say they are not going any more because it is all singing. I work hard for the Lord and I love every minute of it, but it really gets me down when men are keeping away because we are NOT preaching the gospel. It's ridiculous or is it just my problem, Max?

He compensated for the lack of preaching in the chapel by sharing even more with cell mates, especially those who were slow to read or write. 'Tell us the stories of Jesus' they'd ask, 'in your own words'. Malcolm spent hours relating the familiar New Testament stories, sometimes reading them directly from his now tattered Good News Bible. He taught them how to pray, when to pray, and what to pray for. Many came to him asking him to pray with them or for them and some committed their lives to Christ during that time. Pete was one such man.

During free time one day Pete came to talk to Malcolm about a matter that concerned him greatly. He had received a visit from his wife who had told him that the electricity was due to be cut off the following day if she didn't pay the bill. She had no source of income; Pete had none, and she and the children were likely to freeze without heat and light or source of cooking. He felt helpless and extremely anxious. The burden weighed heavily, especially as he wanted desperately as a new Christian to do right by his wife. Malcolm read to him the part of Matthews gospel that Max had read to him that day in the Bradford cell about God providing all our needs. Then they prayed together. Having given the whole matter over to God, Pete left.

Some days later he came running up to Malcolm clutching a letter from his wife. As she had been walking down the street the day following her visit to prison, an old friend of Pete's stopped and gave her some money he had owed him from some time ago. It was enough to pay the bill and buy food for the children. Malcolm and Pete worked out that the incident had occurred at the precise time of their praying together.

Pete was overjoyed and spent the rest of the day telling his friends that God had provided for his family in a miraculous way. A couple of days later he reappeared at Malcolm's door with Keith, another inmate, and the request, 'Malcolm will you pray with Keith, he has debts of £250?!' After Malcolm had explained that the gospel and prayer was a little more than simply praying for money, Keith got his prayer.

As time went on Malcolm received great strength and fellowship from his new converts. Will Barker was now visiting not only Malcolm but several of the men who had received Christ as their Saviour. He brought into the prison Christian films for them to watch and books for those who could read, but above all he prayed for them and with them. The discussion groups grew and became a recognised and established part of prison life for many of the men in Haverigg. Between them, Malcolm, Will and Max linked up prisoners with local church ministers and members in their home town ready for when they got out. Malcolm recognised the help and support that he had gained from Max and was eager to see every man given this opportunity.

Not all who attended the group meetings were believers, but everyone would contribute to the many and varied topics of discussion. Mindful always of the need for these men to one day live in the outside world, Malcolm's view of life and choice of discussion topics was never restricted to just prison.

Max regularly fed Malcolm with details of current affairs, especially national concerns, ranging from the killing of Liverpool policemen, to Northern Ireland; disaster in Pakistan to more local events such as his own parish mission. The men held regular prayer meetings for this Bradford church and made sure that all denominational services in the prison were praying for it.

As the sentence dragged on Malcolm found life on the inside a struggle. He loved witnessing and sharing with the men but not all of them were quite so determined as him to keep the faith. There were weeks when he felt he was moving backwards, not forwards. The ridicule from others was unrelenting and a sense of helplessness came over him as he fought to keep his brothers in Christ on the right track. 'How I wish I were more experienced in the ways of God' he cried to Max, adding 'Do you ever get impatient with God? I've been praying for a particular answer for weeks now, but still nothing'.

There were darker times to come. He feared the time when he would be released and the problems that would inevitably follow. While he was on the inside alcohol ceased to be a problem but he knew he had to face it, and the outside world, in the near future. The closer that time came, the darker he felt his world was becoming, lying under an overcasting shadow that seemed to be growing by the day. He wrote:

Being an alcoholic or being aware of being an alcoholic is the main thing I have come to accept during this sentence. It was Christ who showed me my weakness and made me aware of the consequences of kidding myself about it. Alcoholism is a disease. The thinking processes of the brain are affected by alcohol in the blood system. This is known as 'alcoholic thinking'. I was thinking alcoholic when I called on you, Max, and though I have now been dry for almost eleven months, occasionally I still think alcoholic. Does this surprise you? I have been pickled in alcohol for years and during that time my thinking did a complete flip. But thanks to the Grace of God it has been reversed again, and I am back to my pre-alcoholic way of thinking. I don't know if this is difficult for you to understand. An alcoholic always procrastinates in everything, whether it be a decision or action. Nobody can know just how dark an alcoholics world is unless he has been there. But I have come out of the darkness and was faced with the Living Light. Christ is the light of the world but to me the most important word is TRUTH, or honesty. Honesty with myself, honesty

with others, but more important with God.
Honesty and alcoholism are opposites. The light
comes when I acknowledge Christ. The truth
comes because I walk in the light and the way
becomes easier because I walk in light and truth.
Perhaps this may help you understand me a bit
better.

Malcolm might well have been free of alcohol, but
other temptations still came his way inside Haverigg.
His earnings were small but he was able at times to save
for a few allowed luxuries. The small group of those
who met to study and pray would also give regularly to
charitable concerns through the prison chaplains. The
total amount may have been pence but none the less
Malcolm considered it a good principle for them to all
adopt, in the hope that it might continue when they got
out. His own downfall on money matters came as a
particular blow to him which he grieved over and
confessed in another letter to Max:

I will start this letter before I lose the urge to tell
you of the stupid weakness I succumbed to without
even thinking. Just before I moved into my single
room I decided that the best thing I could do with
some of my money was to buy a Bible, as the one
you gave me is now held together with a couple of
rolls of Sellotape. Then I was told that I could have
a radio in this room. So what did I do? I signed over
£4.25 and bought a transistor. It wasn't until I had
it in my room that I realised what a weak fool I am.
Even this confession doesn't help much because it
doesn't alter the fact that I fell into one of the
devil's simplest traps. I know I should have used
this money to pay back some of what I've stolen. I
wish sometimes, wrongly of course, that God didn't

prick my conscience so much. Perhaps this will show you what a bad example of Christianity I am, but on the brighter side with God's help I try harder to be a better person.

The tension in Malcolm increased as the time for his release approached. He knew his faith was real and he wanted desperately to continue to walk in God's way. Release would be the biggest test of all, for the failure of the past hung over him like a dark cloud. He knew there had been many occasions when he had genuinely sought work and tried to build up normal, healthy relationships, but everything had gone against him. Why, he feared, should it be any different on this occasion?

In the middle of one of Malcolm's rare despondent moods Will Barker paid him a visit. He had a habit of turning up at the right time and on this occasion he brought some good news. Will had spent the weekend speaking to young people in the Midlands, in Nuneaton, at a Christian community called Lindley Lodge. It was an exciting place made up of a varied age group of people whose common link was their faith. Each one gave willingly of their time and skills with view to providing a place for young people to come and discover something of their own personalities and gifts. The warden of this community, Rev. John Moore, was willing to consider Malcolm for a place working with the community on the estate team. It would provide him with accommodation, food, work and the chance to live with a group of Christian people whose lives where committed to serving God .

Malcolm could hardly believe his ears. It was everything he needed, everything that he had feared he would never get. He couldn't wait to tell Max all about it and ask him to pray that God would lead and guide him on this decision. Every part of him wanted to say "Yes" right away, but he knew this was an opportunity that he couldn't afford to blunder. He had to take time to think, pray and consider all that it involved. Part of that process involved a visit to the Midlands.

Within a few weeks Malcolm found himself travelling alone on public transport from Haverigg to Winson Green Prison in Birmingham, where he stayed overnight in order to meet John Moore and the rest of the community. It was the 21st birthday of one of the girls. Malcolm thrived on the happy and relaxed atmosphere as he mingled with the community. All of them were disappointed when the prison wouldn't grant him permission to stay for the evening party. Nevertheless, the outcome was positive, the start of his new life on the outside of prison never, he thought, to return again. In his last letter from Haverigg he records:

> I am safely back from Lindley Lodge and pleased to say I have been accepted by the community there. What a wonderful set of young people they are. I was put at ease as soon as I arrived and made to feel really welcome. What I did notice was that they accepted me as a Christian and not an ex-con. This has never happened before, possibly because I have never met anyone apart from in my prison uniform. It was absolutely marvellous and I am looking forward to going on the 21st of next month (October). I am sure that all that has happened to me since last September has been under the loving guidance of God's hand. How else can I explain it?

I don't pretend to know very much about how or why God does what he does, but I do know with a cast-iron certainty that since being introduced to Jesus Christ my whole attitude to life has changed.

This will probably be my last letter to you from here. There is a certain custom in prison that anyone going out leaves a 'dropsy' to the lads who have been close to him. I will be buying 20 or 30 cigarettes to hand round next week, so I will not be buying any more letters. Anyway I shall try harder and harder for a closer fellowship with God in these last few weeks. Thank you for showing me how to become a Christian, Max. It seems such a long time since I was asking to see you in the police cells in Bradford. So much has changed for me since then. It is with much joy that I look forward to seeing you and Will on the 21st. Thank you for all your prayers, and your letters without which, who knows?

Every blessing,

Malcolm

On October 21st 1971 at 6.30 am Malcolm Worsley was released from Haverigg Prison at the end of his seventh and last sentence. Waiting to greet him and drive him down to Lindley Lodge in The Midlands were his two most treasured friends and brothers in Christ, Will Barker and Max Wigley. Joe Isaacs, the Anglican prison chaplain invited them all to breakfast before setting off on their journey. He greeted Malcolm warmly at the vicarage door with, 'Welcome Malcolm. Call me Joe now.'

Seven

Lindley Lodge

Lindley Lodge in Nuneaton, Warwickshire, first opened as a Christian community and conference centre in 1970. In recent years the large house and estate has been sold to a Christian youth organisation called Youth With A Mission (YWAM). The specialist work of Lindley Lodge now continues at two other centres bearing the same name, one in Masham, North Yorkshire, and the other in Sheffield, South Yorkshire. The commitment to community life at all of the Lindley Lodge centres is of great importance and an integral part of the philosophy of life that it tries to convey to its visitors.

The mixed group of people living and working in the large house and grounds on the outskirts of Nuneaton in the seventies took that responsibility seriously. They aimed to provide a safe, secure and happy environment where young people could come and explore something of their personal attitudes towards work, leisure and the community in which they lived. Some members of the resident community offered their domestic skills, working on the teams responsible for the day-to-day running of the centre. Others worked in administration or on the estate buildings, while a number of others were employed specifically for their teaching and group work expertise – used in planning and leading the various courses. Their gender, marital status, age and experience of life varied, but they all shared a common belief in the Christian way of living and sought to live that out in their work and leisure as members of the community.

Malcolm had been accepted as a member of the team responsible for looking after the twelve-acre estate, including a large house which at that time accommodated up to 75 guests. He was sent with the backing and prayers of Haverigg's chaplain who had grown to know and respect his faith during his ten-month stay. In a letter of commendation to Lindley Lodge's warden, John Moore he wrote:

> As I look back on my four years as chaplain here, with many men coming and going, and often returning, Malcolm's Christian witness has been outstandingly strong and effective. He has been devout and regular in worship, helpful in discussion groups (his hunger to learn is insatiable), and he has a special gift for recruiting and persuading others on behalf of his Lord. I pray he will be able to deal with temptations which will now come, but I am confident that he is capable of good work at counselling and encouraging others.

Will Barker was loved and respected by the community at Lindley Lodge and his confidence in Malcolm had been a great influence in their decision to receive him into the community. John Moore prepared everyone as much as he felt able and right to do. The weekend visit had gone well and left little doubt in any of their minds as to the sincerity and determination of this man to make a new life for himself. They were united in the decision and prayerfully committed themselves to supporting and encouraging the newest member of their community.

Nobody was more aware of Malcolm's need of a family support at that time than Will Barker. He felt sure that God had provided in abundance for Malcolm in the community at Lindley Lodge but had no intention of withdrawing his own support. There would be times when he needed to get away from the larger community and be part of a smaller, more intimate family structure. Thus Will, his wife and children all extended an open invitation to their home whenever Malcolm needed it. On off-duty days, weekends and holidays many of the community would go to be with their families, while Malcolm went to be with his own adopted family, the Barkers.

The arrival of Malcolm on 21st October 1971 remains vivid in the memories of the community who were there to greet him. Will Barker's familiar car with three men inside drew up outside the main entrance in the early afternoon. A small, pathetic-looking figure dressed in old, tattered clothes climbed out clutching two dirty paper carrier bags. There was no mistaking Malcolm. But as he lifted his head, there came a radiance from his eyes that was piercing; a gaze that expressed hope and eagerness. The smile that broke out across his scarred, pitted face relaxed them all. It was crystal clear to everyone that here was a man resolved to take every opportunity that this new life afforded him, and they felt privileged and delighted to be part of that process.

Community life became far more than a process to Malcolm. They became his family, a family lovingly given by God in which he could grow and flourish. Malcolm knew that he had so much to learn and wanted to go back to the very beginning and start life again as a child of God. Just as in any ordinary human family receiving a new baby there were adjustments to make, a lot of giving and taking, loving and forgiving. But there were also rewards and benefits for everyone.

All who knew Malcolm grew to love him and embraced him in the family of Lindley Lodge. Each had a part to play in the rebuilding and restoring of his new life, and their collective influence was to become the foundation upon which he would base the rest of his life. He eagerly studied each member and sought to imitate and adopt the Christlike qualities that he saw. He was never frightened to ask questions, invite criticism, or challenge his teachers should he think them wrong. In their grace and love they gently led and guided, careful never to push for fear of crushing this child of Christ in a man's body.

There was an understandable nervousness among the community in the early days, despite the fact they had done everything possible to welcome him. Pat had lovingly placed fresh flowers in his room, a gesture so small to her but gigantic in his eyes. No-one had ever given him flowers before, and they became the start and a symbol of Pat's inner beauty and friendship, which he would always treasure. 'I've got a lot of bubbles of happiness inside me Malcolm,' she would say, 'and God wants me to share them with you.' Malcolm and Pat became brother and sister right from the beginning. Others were quick to follow.

The paper carrier bags he was holding on arrival contained all his worldly possessions: a Bible, a few letters and documents, a comb, toothbrush and razor. Having lived in prison uniform for so long, he had no clothes. Immediately the men gathered together a few outer garments to tide him over until he earned enough money to buy new ones. Malcolm was overwhelmed by their kindness, deeply moved and grateful for their generosity – but it was the package that lay on his bed on the second day of his stay that caused him to cry.

Placed neatly on his bed were two pairs of new underpants bought and given to him by a fellow member of the estate team. Merv was a joiner with the most brilliant sense of humour and sensitivity. Malcolm hadn't owned any underwear in years, and prison issue were never comfortable. On the outside he'd simply got used to wearing none. The fact that this man had bothered to think or notice this brought tears to his eyes. Receiving this gift was one of the most humbling moments of his life, and he felt flooded with immense gratitude. Merv became one of Malcolm's closest friends. They spent long hours working together on the estate and were never short of conversation or humour. It was with people like Merv that Malcolm found the confidence to talk and even laugh about his own problems. Once, when deeply engrossed in serious conversation about alcoholism, Malcolm looked mischievously at Merv and said, with a twinkle in his eye, 'You see Merv, I had to make a choice between working, or drinking full time; and work seemed to rather get in the way.' There was always a funny side to life for Malcolm, and Merv had a habit of bringing it out in him!

Ian couldn't have come from a more opposite background and life style. He had left a prosperous job and luxurious home to serve on the community of Lindley Lodge. Every advantage and opportunity that life could offer had probably come his way. And yet it was his humility and self-discipline that Malcolm admired. He looked up to him and tried earnestly to imitate the determination and effort he put into Christian discipleship. Ian never stopped working at his faith and, as a direct result of his influence, neither did Malcolm.

Bob became Malcolm's rock. He saw him as Peter the Apostle – solid, dependable, always there and willing to give of himself and his time. As head of the estate team, Bob had immediate responsibility for Malcolm, supervising and overseeing all his work. The community welcomed the tradesman's skills he brought with him, and he became an invaluable resource to them. Not only was he a highly skilled plasterer and bricklayer, but he developed the skills of an instructor always displaying tremendous patience with his new pupils. It was a joy and delight for Malcolm to be able to give something to others in this very practical way. He became a dedicated worker, and the community valued him and his skills enormously.

At first the risk of Malcolm returning to drinking was never far from the minds of the community. Following supper some weeks after his arrival Bob noticed he had disappeared. Feeling confident that he was either working on the estate or taking an early night, Bob joined a group who went off to the local pub for a drink. As they walked through the door, much to their dismay, sitting on a stool at the bar clutching a pint glass was Malcolm. Their hearts sank as they all looked towards him to handle the difficult moment. On closer examination Bob noticed that Malcolm's other hand was holding something else - his open Bible. And the glass contained a pint of Coke. Malcolm had grown impatient with the after-supper chatter, taken himself off to the local church, introduced himself to the vicar and decided to search out the local drunks for a spot of witnessing. He failed to understand the concern or anxiety on the faces of his new family! For them it was a tremendous relief to know that he would be able to take part in the very important social times with the young people in the local pubs without worrying if he would yield to the temptation to drink.

There were however anxious and difficult times ahead. Prison had removed the sight and smell of alcohol and the temptation with it. But every prison sentence had done that, and Malcolm had still returned to heavy drinking soon after each release. Determined as he was on this occasion to stay dry, it didn't automatically relieve his body of the longing for alcohol. The overwhelming urge came to the surface on a number of occasions, and he knew that he had to learn to handle it. It was at times like this that he desperately needed the understanding and patience of his new family. John Moore was among the first to see him through one of these difficult periods soon after his arrival. That particular night Malcolm was wrestling with himself as every part of him craved a drink. He knew that if he remained alone he would lose the battle and so knocked on John and Eileen's front door. Once inside he talked and talked and John listened. When he could talk no more they played table tennis and cards well into the early hours of the morning. Only when John was sure that he had worked through the crisis did he allow him to return to his empty room and be alone. Once there Malcolm turned to his Bible for strength and consolation reading the words, 'I have the strength to face all conditions by the power that Christ gives me.' They were written by his hero Paul who had suffered unbearable beatings and prison sentences for his faith. Holding on to that promise he felt sure that he was going to overcome the alcohol struggle.

Never a day passed when Malcolm wasn't learning new skills for living. Simply waking, dressing, working, talking, eating and playing with others were all major challenges in his life. He threw himself head first into everything and anything he could, barely stopping for a moment in case he missed an opportunity. Sleeping always seemed such waste of time! His enthusiasm once gave him a broken leg during a football game and weeks of misery for the community as they discovered that he was a terrible patient. A pot-legged Malcolm became a comical sight as he hobbled around the estate, determined to keep working. But it was his dress sense that drew the attention of most guests. In direct contrast to the dull grey prison uniform, as soon as his wages allowed him, he bought the brightest and gaudiest coloured clothes he could find. Colour co-ordination was not among his gifts. Many felt he was reflecting his inner happiness on the outside in a very graphic way, while others thought he ought to tone it down a bit!

As the months went by, Malcolm became desperate to work out the right way to live, to find a lifestyle and philosophy that was totally Christian, that would guarantee him 'success' in the ways of God. His first model had been St Paul and now he had John, Eileen, Pat, Bob,

Ian, Merv, Sue and others. But they were all different; some single, some married, from varying backgrounds, Christian traditions and spiritualities. He fought for a clear definition and structure, longing to be the same as those he loved and admired. If only everything could be clear, black and white – but it wasn't. Shirley presented him with his greatest problem so far. She was a wealthy lady. Malcolm decided he had to tell her that it was wrong to be rich as a Christian and that she had no right to own thousands of pounds when there were people hungry and homeless in the world. Shirley invited him to supper one evening in her flat to discuss the problem.

The problem of money was easily resolved in Malcolm's eyes. 'You should just give it all away,' he blatantly informed Shirley. She listened graciously as he off-loaded all his bitterness and resentment towards all who were anything but working-class or poor. He pronounced judgement on any Christian who dare store more than a week's wages or own anything other than life's bare essentials. He knew what it was like, how little one needed to live off, and he would show them how to manage. In fact, at that time, Malcolm thought he had the answers to most problems.

When he had finished his speech, in her own quiet, gentle and loving way, Shirley asked where he might have been now if it hadn't been for Lindley Lodge. He admitted that he wasn't sure what would have happened to him. She pointed out that places like this demanded capital investment and asked him how he would decide between the kind of investment where the 'results' would perhaps be unknown, or in feeding a few hundred hungry people in the world. He went very quiet.

She asked him whether he would give thousands of pounds away in one fell swoop or invest so that the money would make more money to give over a longer period of time. Malcolm lowered his head. Shirley asked him if he would like the responsibility of deciding, when hundreds of needs became known to her, which needy cause she should give to and which to turn down. Malcolm's silence said it all. Shirley offered him the responsibility that accompanied wealth, and he shied away feeling inadequate and daunted.

Malcolm came away indebted to Shirley for yet another important lesson in life. He had taken one more step along the road towards understanding that everyone's circumstances were different and all are called to be a good steward of what God has given them. He had no right to judge anyone else and was learning to appreciate that no two people were the same. He was also discovering that he was an individual, unique in personality and gifting and it was all God-given. He had to learn what was right for himself, not only in the area of stewardship but the whole shape and direction of his life's work. That life work began at Lindley Lodge.

The evening in the pub was the start of regular visits to Nuneaton town although not always to the same place. Clutching his tattered New Testament, Malcolm walked the streets and parks searching out the homeless. He knew where to find them, how they felt, spoke a language that they understood and loved them dearly. The gospel that Malcolm proclaimed was for the lost, lonely and homeless, and it spoke to their bodies, minds and spirits. He talked to the unlovely, wept with those who hurt, befriended those whom society had rejected and where possible fed the hungry. Some he even brought home with him to the Lodge, expecting others to accommodate their many needs as he did. He had no idea of the problems he created and the disruption to community life! Sensitively and with care not to squash the growing concern Malcolm was so obviously developing for the homeless, the community gently reminded him of the main ministry of Lindley Lodge and his job within it. Eager as he always was to learn, he understood and accepted the position, agreeing to restrict his male visitors to his own room and females to the room of any girl in the community who was willing to take them. And all of this had to be in his own time.

Maureen was one of the first young girls he tried to help. Rumour had it that she was living rough and sleeping among the bushes in the local park. No one could persuade her to come out. The nights were getting dark and cold, and there was tremendous concern for her health and well-being. Accompanied by one of the girls from the Lodge, Malcolm sat on a park bench talking in a loud voice, 'I know you're there, Maureen. I don't want to hurt you, just help you. Why not come out and have some soup that I've brought for you.' There was no response. After several attempts he left the flask on the bench, telling her to help herself and he would come back later. It worked, and the pattern continued for several nights. Maureen would drink the soup, eat some sandwiches and return the empty flask for Malcolm to collect later. This long-drawn-out process paid off eventually, as her confidence grew until she felt able to trust Malcolm sufficiently to face him. A very scared, dirty and hungry young girl appeared from the bushes. She was scantily dressed with a face plastered in black mascara. There was little doubt that she would not have survived many more days and nights in those conditions. Maureen was the first of many to be on the receiving end of the love and hope expressed in Malcolm. She accompanied them back to Lindley Lodge, where she shared a single room with one of the secretaries for three to four months.

Such caring was a natural and spontaneous part of his being and part of the new Malcolm who was emerging from within Lindley Lodge. His personal growth and new understanding of life was refreshing and challenging to everyone who worked with him. He became a much-loved and valued member of the community, working not only on the estate team but later as a group leader and tutor on the courses. The transition from the estate to the training side was gradual. At first he would accompany small groups on outdoor activities, giving support and encouragement in an informal atmosphere. But it quickly became clear that Malcolm had an understanding and empathy with the young people that could be used in other areas too. His skill in relating to the youngsters was invaluable, and in time he became a much appreciated tutor.

While the primary aim of Lindley Lodge was not evangelism, the Christian way of life and prayer foundation laid down by members of the community gave rise to many opportunities for faith sharing. Malcolm took every opportunity he could. The place was unimportant – a pub, the coffee bar, disco dance floor or simply walking and talking. Somehow Malcolm found a way to speak for his God. Sometimes his reputation went before him, and one or two youngsters anticipated the challenge with mixed emotions. On one occasion a rather extrovert green-haired young man made his feelings quite clear. 'You're not going to tell me about Jesus, are you?' he challenged Malcolm.

'Not unless you want me to,' came the reply. Nothing else was said about the subject for the next four days until the youth suddenly declared, 'I know you're only waiting for an opportunity to tell me about Jesus, so get on with it!' Malcolm did. Some five or six days later, at the end of the course, the group was enjoying the final disco when the same young man approached Malcolm on the dance floor. He seemed unaware of the booming record blaring out of the speakers as he spoke to Malcolm. 'I've just been upstairs in your chapel –I've never known so much love from people before - I want your Jesus!' Unable to wait until the record was finished or find a suitable, quiet place to talk, he dropped to his knees on the dance floor and asked Malcolm to pray with him. It was Malcolm's joy and privilege to do so.

Life was full at Lindley Lodge, and Malcolm loved every minute of it. In between working and witnessing he still found time to spend in Nuneaton working on the streets and in the pubs, his desire to reach the homeless now increasing by the day. Members of the community encouraged him, and some accompanied him, eager to learn from Malcolm's expertise. One of his most frequent companions was the secretary who had so willingly shared her room with Maureen. She was called Jennifer.

Eight

Jennifer

Jennifer Spensley grew up in some of Cumbria's most beautiful countryside. The small country town of Appleby was an idyllic setting with a strong, stable community life in which children and young people thrived. Their world was tranquil and privileged, rarely touched by the troubles and traumas of the outside world. The Spensley family was respectable and hardworking and well thought of by the local people. The behaviour of the children both inside and outside the home mattered a lot to their parents, and great emphasis was placed upon good behaviour and impeccable manners. Appearances mattered in a close-knit community like Appleby, and the family strived at all times to maintain a good reputation.

As the years went by Mr and Mrs Spensley had good reason to be proud of their children, with one son at Cambridge, a daughter at London University, and Jennifer – while not so obviously academic – clearly making a career for herself, first as a legal secretary, and later as a teacher. Harold, the youngest child, was born mentally handicapped, unable to speak. The family, especially Jennifer who stayed at home longer than her brother and sister, were devoted to caring for him. It was a close-knit and secure family for Jennifer.

As churchwarden Mr Spensley ensured that his children had a Church of England upbringing. Both Jennifer and her younger sister Rachel attended church regularly each Sunday and were familiar with basic Christian teachings and church festivals. But their commitment to church and God was more out of respect and obedience to their parents than religious fervour or spiritual hunger. It wasn't until the physics teacher at school invited them to mid-week Bible studies that they realised that there was any more to Christianity than sitting through a weekly service.

At first attending the group was a novelty, one of the rare 'social' outings that their strict upbringing allowed and therefore not to be missed! But as time went on they began to learn about and understand the Bible in a way that they had never been taught in all their days of churchgoing. The Christian life was explained to them as a relationship with a person rather than a set of rules and code of behaviour. It demanded a response from them. The Bible studies then led them on to young people's camps, where they joined others in the exciting discovery of a personal relationship with Jesus. As teenagers both Rachel and Jennifer committed their lives to God, promising to seek his guidance and leading at every important stage of their lives.

It was a clear call from God over ten years later that brought Jennifer to Lindley Lodge. Following some years working in Edinburgh, training to teach in Huddersfield and a teaching post in Desford, Leicester, she was invited by John Moore to join the community as his secretary. It was a costly decision, but there was no doubt in Jennifer's mind that this was the right one. The sacrifice of a secure career, a teacher's salary, and the freedom and privacy of her own home and life paled into insignificance in the light of God's new direction for her work and life at Lindley Lodge.

Her parents were mystified by their daughter's change of direction, but Rachel, who had shared digs with Jennifer in Leicester, supported and encouraged her in her decision, firmly believing God had called her to work there. They spent a happy Christmas together as a family in Appleby before Jennifer moved out ready to start work in January.

Malcolm had been part of the community for just three months. Jennifer's immediate attraction towards him as a person was not unusual. His warmth, sincerity and magnetic personality had attracted community and guests alike. Still unsure of what might be 'acceptable' social skills, Malcolm had decided it was far easier to display his loving heart to all he met, regardless of who they were or what the occasion might be. Consequently many lives were automatically drawn towards him. Jennifer was no exception.

His dramatic testimony to the power of God in his life left this quiet country girl quite speechless. She'd never heard anything like it. He was the living miracle that she'd always been sure God could perform, the sort of experience she'd read about in Christian books but never met firsthand before now. She listened to his every word and became fascinated by his tales. He was so honest and sincere about his faith. His commitment to God was one hundred per cent and his life totally dedicated to the task of telling others about Jesus. That in itself was appealing to her. Jennifer found that she could talk to him quite openly and freely about many different things without embarrassment. He made her feel safe and secure and became a real rock on whom she learned to rest and depend in times of need. She was a highly gifted and able person in her own right, yet in this man she saw qualities and resources that she loved and valued. And more important than anything else, he had the most brilliant sense of humour! Malcolm never lost an opportunity to joke or tease and frequently provoked endless times of laughter through his own infectious giggle. Their friendship blossomed in this lovely environment of work, play and prayer.

What emerged in time as a two-way attraction did not go unnoticed. Community members and guests often commented on the quality of their working relationship and friendship. The intensity of community life, working, living and socialising together meant that personal relationships often developed very quickly. Jennifer had not realised just how quickly and deeply Malcolm's affection for her had grown until just a few months after her arrival he appeared in her office one day with an attractively-wrapped present.

The watch was beautiful: small, delicate and very feminine. It had cost him all he had managed to save since arriving at Lindley Lodge. This overwhelming expression of affection from Malcolm spoke volumes and caused Jennifer to think seriously about her own feelings towards him. At that time she felt unable to return the same degree of affection openly but was very concerned not to cause him any hurt or sense of rejection. She knew that the watch had cost him far more than just money. In the giving of that gift Malcolm had given part of himself.

It would have been difficult to distance herself from him in the community, and Jennifer had no desire to do that, though she realised it was important that their time together became increasingly work-based, with less time spent alone socially. Working with Malcolm in the evenings provided the ideal opportunity for this. More often than anyone else in the community, she joined him night after night walking the streets of Nuneaton searching out the homeless and needy. If her love for him was to grow, she was confident that it would find the necessary time and space in their work together.

There was so much to learn from this man. She didn't want to miss a thing. Her sheltered upbringing had protected her from any knowledge, let alone sight, of the homeless, alcoholics and prostitutes. She envied Malcolm's understanding, his ability to communicate and the deep compassion he had in his heart for them. At first she watched carefully, learning about their sad conditions, but as time went on she became deeply involved and committed to helping many. They came to trust her and depend upon the friendship and acceptance that she offered alongside Malcolm. They made an excellent team, each needing the other as they worked with both men and women. Their commitment to the work and to one another increased by the day, reaching the stage a few months later when Jennifer welcomed an invitation to spend a day out together in the Lake District. No doubt the Lake District has been the backdrop for many a romance and proposal of marriage with its vast expanses of lakeland water and aspiring hills. But it wasn't Malcolm's choice of scenery on this particular day. The all-too-familiar view of Haverigg prison became the background for their leisurely walk. As they wandered hand in hand along the beach overlooking the dunes and daunting prison complex, Malcolm invited Jennifer to accept his invitation of marriage. Without hesitation, she said yes.

She was twenty-eight years old and very much in love. Even with the prison building dominating the scene, thoughts of Malcolm's past were far from her mind. Jennifer's eyes looked only to the future. Beyond Lindley Lodge that future was unknown, but the strength and security this couple found in each other and in God gave them confidence and courage to look ahead. Being married to Malcolm, she thought, her future was forced to be different – a challenge, a journey of faith and adventure. That sunny July afternoon became the start of an adventure that would bring them back to the small Cumbrian town of Haverigg more times than they could ever imagine.

After choosing a small and inexpensive ring (priceless to them) from a local jeweller's shop, Jennifer and Malcolm drove the short distance to her parents' home in Appleby. Naturally nervous of their response, Malcolm was eager to do everything correctly and in order: so he decided to ask Mr Spensley formally for his daughter's hand in marriage. While Jennifer had spoken to her parents about Malcolm's wonderful testimony, they did not fully appreciate the details of his past. They saw no advantage in hiding the facts and so decided that Malcolm should tell them everything.

Sensing an air of importance about the visit, Mr Spensley invited Malcolm into the front room, leaving Jennifer and her mother alone together in the living-room. Malcolm began his tale looking carefully for indications of approval or disapproval. Neither was forthcoming. On the surface Mr Spensley seemed to be receiving it all without difficulty, but Malcolm knew that it was a lot for any devoted father to take on board in one hearing. Wherever possible he tried to emphasise the future, his commitment to Jennifer and their desire to serve God together. He spoke for some time without being interrupted. However, Mr Spensley continued to listen, nodding occasionally but saying nothing.

Malcolm was left feeling confused and unsure of what reaction he was getting, hoping for the best but fearing the worst. The bemused couple left the family home a short time later feeling they had done all they could but knowing that while disapproval had not been openly expressed neither had the slightest hint of approval been given. As they drove down the motorway they suspected that heated words were being exchanged in the household at that very moment. Only time would tell.

Having decided not to allow the limited response of her parents to dampen their special day, they drove enthusiastically back to Lindley Lodge to share their happy news. The reaction couldn't have been more different. Shrieks of delight, hugs and kisses, and celebrations went on all around the house. Few were surprised and everyone was overjoyed for the happy couple.

The bubble of happiness in Malcolm's and Jennifer's lives burst quite suddenly only a few days later. Arriving by first-class delivery came a carefully constructed letter from her parents. The contents were bold, leaving no doubt whatsoever as to their feelings and intentions concerning the proposed marriage. As far as they were concerned, it was quite out of the question; and they intended to enlist the support of as many senior people they could, including the Bishop of Coventry, to ensure that the marriage didn't take place. Letters to these people had already been sent.

The letter fulfilled their worst fears and stunned them into silence. Slowly the tears began to fall, not out of anger or bitterness, but out of a deep sense of sorrow and compassion for two loving and protective parents. They understood their fears, some of which were shared by others. Malcolm's own mother had cautiously reminded Jennifer of the hurt and pain he'd caused his first wife and sons. Jennifer was not blind to the difficulties she knew she would face living with a man bearing the scars of an alcoholic, still a heavy smoker, and living with the ghost of a criminal record. They were real problems, and she knew they wouldn't go overnight, but God had promised, 'I will never leave you, I will never abandon you!', and that was a promise she knew would carry her through. What she hadn't been prepared for and could well live without was this direct opposition from her family at the start. Malcolm was a new creation, and she longed for them to see him in that light.

Despite letters and visits from Jennifer and other supportive people attempting to play go-between there was no changing her parents' minds. Attempts on their part to enlist the support of senior officials in the church had failed. Eventually the wedding date was fixed for Sunday September 24th at Kirby Muxlow Baptist church.

There was no shortage of enthusiasm and helpers. Preparations for the day became the joy and delight of the entire community. Planning the catering, transport, photography, flower arranging, cake decorating, music, and finding a best man, sidesmen and bridesmaid involved just about every individual at Lindley Lodge. The wedding dress was made by a dear lady who had been one of Malcolm's first Sunday school teachers as a young child. On learning of his faith and transformation, she wanted also to contribute towards the special day. Will Barker, Malcolm's faithful prison visitor and friend, was given the greatest honour of all – to give the bride away. He had been more than a father to this couple and shared fully in their joy and delight on this tremendous occasion. Jennifer's family support at the service came from a few aunts and her sister Rachel, who had married earlier that summer. She stood by Jennifer, in every respect, as her matron of honour.

Over a hundred guests crowded into the small chapel that Sunday afternoon. It was harvest festival weekend, and the whole building was decorated with fruits, flowers and vegetables – a beautiful sight. The ceremony was bound to be different simply by its circumstances, but there was no doubt in anyone's mind just how different it was going to be when the Bridal March struck up on the organ. As Jennifer appeared at the top of the aisle, arm linked to Will, the impatient groom decided he was going to meet his bride halfway. Turning in full view of the congregation Malcolm walked swiftly down the aisle taking Jennifer by the hand and leading her back to the front of the church. There wasn't a dry eye in the church.

Accompanied by a community member on the guitar the congregation stood to sing 'Amazing Grace! How sweet the sound that saved a wretch like me. I once was lost but now am found. Was blind but now I see.' God's grace abounded that day as two very special people were joined together in marriage by God.

The newlyweds' first home was a small flat within the estate reserved for married couples serving the community. During the day their work continued on the team and in the office, and where possible the evenings were spent working together on the streets of Nuneaton. Being married gave Malcolm and Jennifer additional freedom in helping the homeless. Their increased joint income and flat enabled them to offer practical help in terms of clothing, food, warmth and shelter. Very soon they were accommodating a homeless man and woman, Bob and Maureen. There was no extended honeymoon. Life was full and busy, but everything that they had ever wanted. The discovery, rather more quickly than expected, that Jennifer was pregnant, added to their joy. The honeymoon baby was expected in June 1973.

There was only one name both of them wanted for their firstborn, namely Paul after St Paul, the life of whom had influenced Malcolm only two years earlier. His arrival was surrounded with joy and happiness not least because of the reconciliation that the pregnancy had brought between the Worsleys and the Spensleys.While Jennifer had continued to write regularly since the wedding, informing her parents of all that was happening in their lives, it was the news that they were about to become grandparents that had softened their hearts. Seeds of healing and reconciliation were sown and grew steadily as the years passed. (During Mr

Spensley's very serious illness nearly twenty years later he asked to speak with Malcolm alone. The two were more than father and son-in-law; they had become friends and soulmates. He died just a few months later.)

The Worsley household now totalled five. Jennifer endeavoured to feed, clothe and accommodate them all, fitting in additional duties in the community wherever possible. Transformed from an alcoholic to a workaholic, Malcolm packed in as many hours as he could on the streets and in the pubs. Their deep concern for the homeless increased by the day.

Local churches in Nuneaton were well aware of the presence of Lindley Lodge and welcomed the opportunities for ecumenical contact that it offered them. Malcolm was especially keen to build stronger links between the denominations, uniting all Christians in the task of bringing the gospel to the whole town. He made every effort to inform and involve any who showed an interest in his work on the streets and regularly spoke to church groups about the work.

Part of his ecumenical involvement took both him and Jennifer, just a few months after Paul was born, to London to attend a national conference on evangelism. The well-known evangelist, Dr Billy Graham, spoke powerfully of the need for local churches to respond to the glaring conditions of the socially deprived in the country, especially the homeless. At the end of the evening he invited people to commit themselves publicly to this work. Separated by thousands of people across the vast auditorium in Earls Court, both Jennifer and Malcolm stood to commit their lives to reaching the homeless and needy wherever and however God should lead them. It was only later that evening that each told the other of their response. Paul, just three months old and fast asleep in his push-chair, was also to become an integral part of that family ministry.

As they journeyed home to the Midlands at the end of the week, they knew that the last few days had become a turning point in their lives and ministries. What the future held they didn't know, but the one thing they both felt sure of was that the time had come, however painful it might be, to break away from their family at Lindley Lodge.

Nine

St James, Weddington

Guy Cornwall-Jones had been the rector of St James, Weddington, since 1964. While he was studying English at Cambridge he came to a personal faith in Christ during a university mission. This was the first of many led by a London-based clergyman called John Stott. Thus after Cambridge Guy offered himself for ordination training and soon returned to college to study theology.

St James was his first church and his first opportunity to put into practice all he had learned. A small but determined nucleus of people made up the congregation, but the first seven years were an uphill struggle. Lindley Lodge was on the parish boundary and so a 'two-way street' between Guy and the community naturally developed. Guy received encouragement and fellowship there, and individual members of the community joined the worshipping congregation of St James.

The first of these was David, a mechanic in his early twenties, who had met the Holy Spirit in a powerful way. Through prayer and Bible reading he brought a special ministry of prophecy and encouragement to the church family. At the same time Guy was also helped by a travelling preacher from the Plymouth Brethren church called Peter Brandon. Through Peter's teaching ministry, he came to a deeper understanding of the work of the Cross in his own life – one that had a powerful impact on his ministry. God was preparing him individually and the St James people corporately for an important time ahead.

It was nearly two years later in January 1973, a few months alter marrying Jennifer, that Malcolm first had clear guidance from God to join St James, Weddington. 'God has sent me to join your church,' he told the tall, refined English vicar as he stood on the vicarage doorstep. Of course it wasn't the first time Malcolm had made bold declarations on vicarage doorsteps but, at least, on this occasion, he wasn't quite such a risk! Guy responded politely by inviting him in and went on to share with him all that God had been saying to them as a church in the last two or three years. Malcolm identified strongly with part of the prophetic word they were hearing and felt sure he had a very specific part to play in the life of this church family. Then in his own time he shared with Guy his vision for reaching people in body, mind and spirit, especially the homeless. All his concerns were very close to the things that God had laid on Guy's heart.

As the weeks and months progressed Guy became Malcolm's confident, listening carefully to many of his present frustrations. He felt called to be his Barnabas, introducing him to the other apostles, encouraging and releasing his friend into a wider ministry. He wondered if Malcolm ought to have more training from others with greater experience of working with the homeless. With this in mind, he arranged a trip to St George's church in Leeds, where he knew there was an extensive ministry going on among the 'down and outs' in the city. This would provide an opportunity for Malcolm to see a different situation and allow him to test his calling for the work in Nuneaton. During the journey the two men relaxed and chatted about a number of things, not least their vision for the future. On their way home they stopped at a service station and Guy drew Malcolm's attention towards a smart Jaguar. As they stood admiring the car's sleek lines, they commented on the unusual licence plate – ACT 132B. Guy smiled and suggested light-heartedly that it could be a Bible reference. Opening his New Testament in the car, Malcolm turned to the Acts of the Apostles, 13:2, and read the second half of the verse 'Set apart for me Barnabas and Paul for the work to which I have called them'. There was now no doubt in Guy's mind that he and Malcolm were to work together and that they were in the right place.

Malcolm and Guy met regularly to pray together on Saturdays at 6am. It was during this time that they developed a vision for a united church work in Nuneaton. Even in his prison days Malcolm had never seen much point in denominations and worked tirelessly, if with little success, to unite the different services there.

In Nuneaton there were thriving congregations of Baptists, Wesleyan Reform, Roman Catholics, Anglicans, URC, Pentecostals, Methodists and Plymouth Brethren. The two men felt sure that if these people could be united in their vision for the proclamation of the gospel message in Nuneaton, God would do wonderful things.

With this vision Guy and Malcolm invited church leaders from all the denominations to meet at Lindley

Lodge. An open, warm spirit of sharing emerged, during which time the Plymouth Brethren told of their plans for an Easter mission in 1974. The preacher invited was Peter Brandon, who had been such a help and encouragement to Guy only a few years earlier. As these leaders talked, prayed and waited on God a clearer vision emerged for a united town-wide mission, and the Brethren offered their plans as a basis for it. The decision was unanimous; prayer and planning began immediately. Quite independently, the Bishop of Coventry, Dr Cuthbert Bardsley, announced his decision to send a four-person team of Church Army evangelists to Nuneaton from September 1973. They soon became an integral part of the mission, and Malcolm emerged as one of several gifted evangelists in the group, as well as an important link between different denominations.

Malcolm was inspired by all these developments but also frustrated. He wanted to devote more and more time to working with the homeless and using his evangelistic gifts locally in the churches. Guy had already welcomed him into the pulpit of St James, where he had shared his testimony and preached the gospel. His study in prison had given him some excellent Bible qualifications which went a long way towards his being considered as a Church of England lay reader. Because of his exceptional background and growing ministry in the diocese, the bishop invited Malcolm to talk with him. A half-hour interview was sandwiched between two other important engagements, so he was quite tired when Malcolm arrived. Fortunately all he had to do on this occasion was listen as Malcolm poured forth the tale of how he had become a Christian and all that God had done in his life since. Cuthbert Bardsley was enthralled and, forgetting his next appointment, encouraged Malcolm to continue his story. After an hour he finally rose to his feet saying, 'What a delight, I must give you a blessing, Malcolm.' He raised his hands and rested them on Malcolm's head. 'May God bless you, Malcolm,' he said. Totally unaware of Anglican ceremony, Malcolm placed his hands on the bishop's head, also saying, 'And God bless you too, bishop.' A delighted Cuthbert Bardsley flung open the doors to his study declaring to his next visitor, 'How wonderful, I've just been blessed. Bishops need blessings too. How wonderful!' The two men were to meet on many occasions in the future and always delighted in remembering the day the bishop received a blessing.

In the midst of the excitement, the changes locally and his search for an answer to present frustrations, Malcolm put a suggestion to Guy. 'Perhaps we should just leave Lindley Lodge and live by faith continuing the work that way?' he said. Guy was cautious in his reply but hinted it might well be a possibility and rather casually admitted that they had been considering sharing their home with other Christians. It was a passing comment, more thinking aloud than a serious offer. He was about to learn something very important about his friend 'Paul', that, given the slightest encouragement, he acted fast.

Only days later Malcolm stood once more on the vicarage doorstep saying, 'Jennifer and I have handed in our notice at Lindley Lodge. When can we move in? Oh, and you were including Maureen and Pat (the most recent additions to their household) in the invitation, weren't you?' Standing listening to Malcolm, Guy struggled to remember if he had even mentioned this passing comment to his wife Helen. Perhaps if he'd deliberated for too long the decision would never have been made, but this, he felt, was just a little too fast! In an attempt to slow down the process slightly the Cornwall-Jones' and the Worsleys agreed to explore and pray through the possibility and practicability of the suggestion. After much deliberation, and to avoid any unreal expectations or false hopes, they finally decided upon a commitment of three months, at the end of which time Malcolm and Jennifer agreed to find alternative accommodation.

By the end of November 1973 the five members of the Worsley household had moved into two rooms at Weddington Rectory. Only a few weeks later they discovered that the sixth member was well on its way; Jennifer was pregnant again, with Paul just five months old.

The urgency to find their own accommodation was increased by the impending birth of a second baby. Guy and Helen were marvellous in sharing their home, never allowing them to feel visitors but always members of this rapidly extending family. Their own first child, Ruth, was just under four years of age. The differing lifestyles took some adjusting to, especially where Maureen and Pat were concerned, but they coped without complaint or ill feeling.

Malcolm was never happier, dividing his time between helping Guy at St James and working on the streets, as well as doing everything that he could towards the Easter mission. Jennifer was naturally tired with a young baby and a second due later that year. She took responsibility for the day-to-day organising of the two girls, encouraging them to share the workload wherever possible. They had no regular income of any kind, living completely by faith, but God never let them down. Many members of St James admired their courage and conviction and regularly provided clothing, gifts of food and sometimes money. Most of all they prayed for them. At other times gifts would appear on the doorstep and through the letter box with no indication of their senders. In Malcolm's and Jennifer's minds this provision confirmed that they were in the right place, doing what God had called them to do.

Their low earnings at Lindley Lodge hadn't given much of an opportunity to save, so looking for a house to buy seemed impossible. Malcolm approached the council about renting a property. It wasn't ideal because of the continual coming and going of homeless girls that they anticipated, feeling sure that the council might object to their property being used in this way. In the event they were indeed refused a council house, but, much to their surprise and delight, were offered instead a 100% mortgage on a property they could buy. It was a miracle! Not only did Malcolm have no regular income with which to repay the mortgage but he could offer no financial guarantee other than confidently telling the council God would provide!

Duke Street was not in the most desirable area in Nuneaton. Its old terraced houses were severely neglected. Because properties were cheaper, many of the Asian community had moved into the district, resulting in a mass exodus of white English occupants. The Worsleys were undisturbed by colour of skin, language or culture. It might not be a palace or particularly fit for human habitation (yet!), but the end terrace on Duke Street was their first house, and they were proud of it. Malcolm thanked God again for the building skills he had acquired early in his life and started on the long task of making the house into a home.

For £1,200 they gained two bedrooms and a bathroom upstairs, two living rooms and a minute kitchen downstairs. The house might not have seemed large to anyone else but to them it was more than double the space they'd had before and therefore allowed for accommodation of double the number of homeless. Together as they tore through endless layers of wallpaper, all seemingly stuck together with garlic and spices, Malcolm and Jennifer decided how they would organise the house. It made sense for them to occupy the two rooms upstairs with Paul and the new baby, while downstairs in one of the living rooms they would place two sets of bunk beds to take up to four homeless girls at any one time. The second living room would double as a dining room, which would no doubt be very crowded at times. The kitchen was the biggest concern, and if Jennifer was going to fit more than herself in it, an extension was needed. The building would be no problem, but finding the time in which to do it might prove difficult. Jennifer knew that Malcolm needed a deadline, so they decided it had to be complete by the time Jennifer came out of hospital with the new baby.

The biggest distraction to building and redecorating was the Easter mission. The United Reformed Church in Nuneaton seated 1,000 people so naturally became the venue for the nightly meetings. A hundred people came on the first night and sat huddled together at the back of the hall. The atmosphere was cold and stilted, leaving the Christians discouraged and confused. They'd been so sure that it was God's will to have a united mission they couldn't understand why the response was so poor. The planning group met to pray the following morning. The outcome was not what any of them had expected or especially wanted, as God seemed to confront them with their divisions and differences. It was indeed a united mission he had wanted, the denominations working together as the one body of Christ. Instead disagreement, pride and deep-seated resentments had to be dealt with.

Malcolm decided to talk about an experience he had had a few weeks earlier. He explained how during the time he had been meeting to pray with a small number of church leaders he had begun to feel strangely on the outside of that group. However hard he tried to push himself into the circle, he remained on the edge. While wrestling in prayer over the matter, he received a clear image in his mind of a large bubble. The bubble was Christ, and within it his group of friends were praying. During the course of the day, as he continued to pray, the bubble slowly absorbed him, and God spoke powerfully about being 'in Christ'. Malcolm then came to a fresh understanding of what being 'in Christ' meant and how his own efforts to be part of the body of Christ had been in vain. Only as he focused on Jesus and submitted totally to him did he feel part of the group around him.

Peter Brandon, leader of the mission, took Malcolm's vision and applied it to what was happening now. He invited the people at the prayer meeting to stand and link hands with their friends around them and then asked if they thought that this was an expression of

Christian unity. Nearly everyone did. Peter observed that the group was looking at each other and quietly suggested that real unity, as Malcolm had discovered, came in looking into Jesus. He asked them to turn inwards and look upwards, focusing on Christ but still linking hands. It became a painful and yet powerful time of learning for them all as God poured his Holy Spirit upon the mission. Each night the numbers at the evening meetings grew until, on the last evening, the hall was packed.

The Christian church in Nuneaton and district grew in numbers and strength. The months and years that followed were a remarkable testimony to renewal and revival with hundreds of individuals committing their lives to Christ and a unity between denominations never previously experienced. Malcolm continued to initiate and lead many inter-denominational gatherings. St James became a centre for renewal through weekly ecumenical praise and worship meetings, sometimes inviting outside speakers and on other occasions using local ministers. One of the most memorable gatherings was the presentation of a popular Christian musical called 'Come Together', in the Baptist Church. Malcolm himself preached to a packed congregation of over a thousand people. His gifts were becoming widely known and used by God. In recognition of his vital part in renewal and evangelism Bishop Cuthbert Bardsley gave him permission to act as an evangelist within the diocese, giving him a wider and more recognised ministry. In place of his blue lay reader's scarf he now wore the bright red scarf of an evangelist, with pride and thankfulness.

With the mission over, kitchen extension completed and baby Helen safely delivered into the world, Malcolm and Jennifer prepared to receive their first new residents into Duke Street. Every one of them came off the streets either through Malcolm's own contacts or by referral from individuals or groups who knew of their work. In later months the official bodies of social and probation services began to seek out Malcolm and Jennifer to reach those whom they could not. Angie was one such, among the first to occupy one of the four bunks in Duke Street's downstairs bedroom. She was just seventeen years old, seven months pregnant, kicked out of home and found living in the back of an abandoned mini van. Malcolm went to try to persuade her to come and live with them. Angie was scared and lonely. She'd heard about 'the vicar' as the street folk of Nuneaton had nicknamed Malcolm but, desperate a she was, had no intention of getting preached at in her condition. Malcolm stood patiently reassuring her and willing her to step out of the van. There was never any active preaching or teaching in the home. Malcolm and Jennifer had decided they simply had to live out their faith, allowing their actions to do the speaking unless directly asked or invited to do otherwise by the girls. On this occasion his patience was rewarded as Angie agreed to accompany him home, where she stayed until her baby was born.

Wherever possible the girls continued in their jobs, contributing to the upkeep of the house when they could. But the majority were unemployed or, as in Carol's case, earned their living through prostitution. Keeping Carol occupied and off the streets wasn't easy. She had come from a wealthy middle-class family where she had been brought up in emotionally sterile conditions. Starved of physical affection and any demonstration of love from either parent, Carol discovered at thirteen that some people did want to touch her. What started as kissing and cuddling behind the bike shed at school had developed into full-scale prostitution by the time she was 15. She became obsessed, often going with five or six men a night, unable to control herself. She hated herself and the obsession that possessed her, often spending hours and hours helplessly crying in the arms of Jennifer or Malcolm. They were probably the only arms she had ever known to offer her unconditional love and acceptance.

There were many times in those early days at Duke Street when Malcolm risked life and limb to protect the girls. Angie came running home one day pleading for him to rescue another of the girls called Sharon who had got herself trapped in a bedroom with four men. Alone and half the height and weight of any of them, Malcolm boldly knocked on the door and demanded to see Sharon. Once the door opened Malcolm could see her sitting half naked and trembling on the edge of a bed. Four men stood between her and the door. 'Jesus loves Sharon and wants her to come home with me,' he said, staring the first youth in the eye. Seemingly without any fear, he walked across the room, instructing Sharon to get dressed quickly and walked out with her just seconds later.

A terrified young girl accompanied him home. It was only later that he himself went into shock, realising the potential danger that they had both been in. On another occasion, they received a young, severely abused Indian schoolgirl who had escaped home and family in fear of an arranged marriage. All of the men in her family descended upon Duke Street to take her home. Malcolm was left with the lonely task of defending her. Many of the girls had been abused physically, and nearly all were scarred emotionally. The majority had also become regular users of ouija boards or other forms of occult practice. Few had known stability or love in their young lives. Duke Street became a place of refuge for dozens and dozens of them in that first year. Some stayed a few nights, others weeks or months. Wherever possible Malcolm and Jennifer encouraged them to rebuild links with their families. Others just needed time and space to work out their problems. There was rarely a night when a bunk remained empty as the needs always outnumbered the beds. Malcolm and Jennifer knew that they were only scratching the surface and as time went on it wasn't only the plight of girls that became the focus of their concern.

The death of an ageing homeless man discovered lying in the backstreets of Nuneaton in a cardboard box in the midst of newspapers and carrier bags shocked the whole town. His left hand had been eaten by rats. The front page headlines of the local paper described the circumstances graphically. Such details were no news to Malcolm, who regularly saw such sights and conditions. But the article had a drastic effect on him. He became desperate to provide some shelter for these men. Duke Street wasn't the place, already too small for the work it had to do, and they would never combine men and girls in the same home. Malcolm began walking the streets to find another place of refuge, this time for men.

Ten

Midland and Oaston Roads

Like so many local authorities, Nuneaton Borough
Council struggled to provide support or make adequate
provision for homeless people in the district. The temptation to pretend that there wasn't a problem, was
always there, until headlines in the local newspaper
faced them with something of the plight of these people. Part of the problem lay in the fact that the people
with the power to influence change rarely saw the
conditions in which homeless people lived. When such
circumstances were brought to their notice, as in the
tragic case of the elderly man, they were considered
extreme, rare and blown up by the press. But Malcolm
knew differently. There were more people living rough
on the streets than even he dared to think of; and the
most vulnerable were the elderly, mentally ill, drug
users and alcoholics. Any kind of shelter found by these
people would be extremely basic; at best a derelict
house and at worst a bus shelter or porch entrance to a
public building. Newspapers, cardboard torn from su-
permarket boxes or plastic carrier bags would become
their only protection from the cold night air. A few
lucky ones might have acquired a blanket or two from
a charity shop or refuse tip, but most were not so

fortunate. Open fires, which frequently endangered not only their own lives but those of others living in nearby properties, were their only source of heat. Derelict buildings were especially dangerous places for the vulnerable homeless.

During the winter months and in severe weather conditions men would gather together, sleeping huddled in small groups, sheltering each other. Many suffered permanently with coughs, colds and other minor ailments but some were more seriously ill. They would end up in the casualty department of the local hospital where they'd at least find warmth, comfort and appropriate treatment. Others would inevitably end up in cells at the local police station. Staff grew familiar with many of the characters and the sense of helplessness in their lives. Malcolm had no need to understand; he knew from firsthand experience what it was like to feel rejected, desperate and alone in the world. Almost five years might have passed since he had walked the streets in search of accommodation and help, but the memory of those days remained crystal clear. He had been given a fresh chance, the opportunity to turn his back on the past and start again, and he longed to give these men the same. He knew that not one of them chose or wanted to live under these circumstances, and, given the opportunity, they could make something of their lives. His task was somehow to provide that opportunity.

Number 3 Midland Road was owned by Nuneaton Borough Council. It was very run down and as far as Malcolm could see hadn't been occupied for some time. With improvements and redecoration he felt sure that it was the perfect place to accommodate homeless men. Before approaching the council, both he and Jennifer prayed. At first the council insisted that it couldn't release a property for this purpose, because the system prevented it. Despite having seen the value of the work at Duke Street and knowing the project at Midland Road was not likely to cost the council anything, councillors still couldn't see a way through the laws and regulations, though they did appear genuinely sorry. Malcolm had little patience with bureaucratic structures at the best of times, but on this occasion he was incensed by the red tape that was preventing them from occupying Midland Road. Then, rather quietly and off the record, somebody muttered something about how difficult and pointless it would be to remove anybody who might choose to occupy it. Malcolm took the hint, left quickly and started to make his plans.

At the St James Wednesday fellowship meeting that week he told them about Midland Road. A special time of praise and thanksgiving was offered to God for that wonderful provision, and together they committed the total needs of that project to God in prayer. Only a few months later Malcolm was informed that under a section of the Public Housing Act of 1936, number 3 Midland Road was now officially available as a 'Common Lodging House'. Both the council and the Worsleys were delighted. Prayer and hard-working solicitors had won the day, moving even borough councils.

With no time to waste Malcolm gathered around him a group of Christian friends who both worked and prayed about the house. It needed plumbing, rewiring, redecorating and at a later date windows were also replaced. Local churches donated mattresses, furniture, pots and pans, clothing and blankets, and within just a few weeks the first six men came to live in Midland Road. The conditions were deliberately basic but adequate. Each came with his own tale, sad circumstances and personal battles to face. Many were alcoholics, some drug users and others suffering from some degree of mental illness. The majority had at some stage been inside prison. The cards were stacked against them, and life was pretty bleak and dark wherever they looked. Midland Road became a small but bright light in that darkness strong enough for some to mark out a new and positive future for themselves. Nothing delighted Malcolm more than to give them that hope.

Midland Road operated an 'open door' policy for twenty-four hours a day. Each man was received and accepted for what he was, not what he had been. Many were rejects from other institutions, and nearly all came in straight off the streets, where they might have been 'dossing' for some time. The rooms within the house varied. Some were as basic as a mattress on the floorboards, others had a bed, while one was eventually carpeted and equipped with several items of furniture. Men were encouraged to choose whatever degree of comfort they felt happy with. Everyone was expected to pay a minimum contribution to cover the cost of electricity, furniture, coal and crockery but they were encouraged to organise the house themselves, even the rent collection. It would become one man's responsibility to collect the money and hand it over to Malcolm at the end of the week. There was rarely an occasion on which a man did not pay his way. The 'self-help' philosophy was an important part of helping the men to regain self-worth and discipline. Malcolm never stayed on the premises for any length of time and disliked the whole concept of staffed hostels. Responsibility was placed upon them, and they were left to work out the day-to-day running of the house alone. As a result house rules emerged from the men themselves and were enforced by them! Inevitably newcomers were treated with suspicion and indifference at first until they showed some willingness to comply with the rules, but in time they too grew to respect the property, its contents and the trust placed upon them. A local Christian even donated a colour television, which in those days was considered quite a luxury, and never once was it abused, damaged or any attempt made to steal it.

Malcolm's role at Midland Road was critical, although he never appeared as a dominant authoritative figure. Every day he walked to the house ready to listen and help where he could.

The men were never quite sure what to make of him, but as time went on it was his empathy, not sympathy, that spoke the loudest. They couldn't fail to recognise that he knew and understood their suffering. His first-hand knowledge and experience of social services, probation services and legal proceedings was invaluable. He spent hours reading and interpreting complicated forms and leaflets. Many of them trusted him with their sad life stories. He accompanied those who were nervous and frightened of facing 'official' bodies or people and represented others who were incapable of speaking for themselves. Malcolm became their confidant and their 'arms', 'legs' and 'voice' when needed. By now his reputation with all of the official bodies in Nuneaton was positive; they had grown to respect and trust him. Earlier in the year, Geoff Ainsworth, the director of Nuneaton Social Services, had given him six months' casual work as a social worker. Now, months later, he was still doing much of the department's work although in an unrecognised and unofficial capacity. Hours of his time were spent in court, probation offices and police stations. On a number of occasions he was able to secure bail for some of the men, giving them time and space to work through many of their problems from Midland Road instead of a police cell.

The ages and circumstances of each man varied considerably. Among the youngest came a 17-year-old who had already spent several years in borstal. The authorities held out little hope for his future with no family or friends to support or encourage him each time he came out. Midland Road provided a base, people who understood, friends and space in which to stand back and reflect upon his circumstances. Nobody had ever offered him these things before. Over a period of months he regained some self-worth and confidence, started to apply for jobs and eventually rented a flat of his own. There was no greater satisfaction for Malcolm than to see the growth and development of this young man and others.

At the other end of the scale came a 67-year-old who, weary of life, simply wanted to die. With no living relatives or local authority help, he had ended up living on the streets. Malcolm found him, and Midland Road became his place of refuge. Months of negotiating and pushing finally secured him a place in a residential home for the elderly, where he ended his days with a degree of dignity and pride instead of becoming simply another statistic on the list of homeless deaths.

Caring for all of these men became a twenty-four hour job with very little time off for Malcolm or Jennifer. He promised them that whenever they needed him he would be there, whatever time of day or night it might be. Bob really tested his endurance. An alcoholic and depressive, as well as desperately insecure, he regularly rang Malcolm, threatening suicide. At varying times of the night and early hours of the morning Malcolm left his bed to sit with him, talking him through his trauma. The pattern repeated itself night after night until Malcolm become exhausted. 'Please, Bob, don't ring me tonight, You'll be all right, I know you will,' he pleaded. At two o'clock the following morning the telephone rang. Malcolm groaned, and Jennifer begged him not to go out again. The all-too-familiar voice spoke on the other end, 'It's me Malcolm, Bob. I'm just ringing to tell you you can stay in bed. I'm all right. Don't worry about coming out tonight as I'm not going to do anything silly, I promise.' Fortunately God had given both Malcolm and Jennifer a helpful sense of humour!

There were many stories of success and failure, but the full impact of Midland Road upon men's lives could never be calculated in quantitative terms. It was impossible to measure the effects of love, concern and compassion. Shelter, beds, clothing and food were essential but temporary. The Worsleys had something that would remain long after the warm fire, hot meal and clean clothes, but they knew it could never be forced onto any one of them; each individual had to want and choose it for himself. Their job was simply to demonstrate it and, when invited, talk about the hope and meaning to life that they had both found through faith in God.

Some scoffed at the spiritual food available, taking all the material and practical help they could get, and then leaving. Others welcomed talk about God and expressed a real interest for a short time but were soon drawn back into the false and temporary world of alcohol, drugs and crime. But there were those who were genuinely seeking for that which would change the direction of their lives, and many found it at Midland Road. Keith was among the first and became a source of real encouragement to Malcolm and Jennifer as they saw this simple man change, growing in love, faith and confidence.

Following the breakdown of his second marriage life seemed pretty meaningless for Keith. With the help of a bottle of whisky and sleeping tablets, he tried unsuccessfully to end it all. It was soon after this that he was introduced to Malcolm through a friend already living at Midland Road. In the weeks and months that followed, Keith made three new friends; Malcolm, Jennifer and God. Walking into their home, playing with the children and being with them as a family was like getting to know God. The unseen person of Jesus was always present, and Keith couldn't fail to notice. He was full of faith and gratitude, doing everything he could to improve conditions at Midland Road for all who lived there. Shadowing Malcolm most of the time, he became his right-hand man, learning all he could from him in the process.

Within a year of their occupying number 3, the borough council announced that the Worsleys could also take over the house next door, provided that it was improved to environmental health standards. Keith carried out a lot of the work on this property and started to take responsibility for the ever-increasing numbers of residents within. He also found casual work as a gardener and saved all but a few pounds of his wage, determined one day to use it to make a new start in life. That opportunity came, again through Malcolm and Jennifer, sooner than he expected.

As well as numbers 3 and 5 Midland Road, Duke Street continued to receive its endless stream of teenage girls, many of whose problems became far more difficult to handle than the men's. Jennifer worked day and night to provide a home for them, sharing not only the house, food and possessions, but herself, her husband and children. With both Paul and Helen growing fast, they began to wonder how much longer they could stay in the small terraced house. Every week they were turning girls away because of lack of space. Even though local Christian groups were providing increased financial support, for Jennifer and Malcolm the possibility of buying a larger property was out of the question. As always they took the problem to God in prayer.

A couple of weeks later Malcolm received a phone call from the rural dean, the Reverend David Jameson. An elderly lady from his congregation had recently died leaving a houseful of furniture. The relatives wanted Malcolm to have first refusal on the house contents for use at Duke Street and Midland Road. It was a tremendous offer, so he arranged to meet a relative of the deceased woman at the house the following day.

The Oaston Road house was a dream. It had five bedrooms, a large kitchen, two reception rooms downstairs and two toilets! Malcolm's mind was severely distracted from the furniture he should have been looking at as he stood trying to imagine what he and Jennifer could do with a place like that. It would allow for a little bit of family privacy, he thought. There was even a self-contained unit within the house where the girls could have a lot more space.

His imagination ran wild until in a typically forthright style Malcolm heard himself say to the relative, 'The house is nice. I don't suppose we could have that as well?' It was more a spoken dream than a serious question, for he knew full well they couldn't afford to rent or buy a house of this size. The response was not at all what he expected. He could hardly believe his ears as the reply came back very calmly, 'I don't see why not. We don't have any immediate plans for it.'

For once in their lives they were speechless. The second property at Midland Road had been an unexpected surprise, but this was more than they could ever ask or imagine. God had gone ahead, paving the way and supplying them with all that they needed to do his work. Malcolm and Jennifer were quick to share the good news with David Jameson, whose delight showed all over his smiling face. He was thrilled to have been able to play a small part in a big miracle. With thanks and praise in their heart, they made immediate plans to move.

Leaving Duke Street and all its memories was made easier by the delight of its new owner, Keith. For many months Jennifer had deposited his wage in a savings account for him, never imagining it would become the deposit for buying his own home. He loved every part of that building, having spent endless happy hours with the extended family there. Keith couldn't believe his ears when the Worsleys offered it to him, and in a short time he had obtained a mortgage. The grand move began; Keith from Midland Road to Duke Street, the Worsleys from Duke Street to Oaston Road.

The Worsleys were working flat out with hardly any time to draw breath as the work both at Oaston Road and Midland Road seemed to be growing by the week. Malcolm was now responsible for three properties, with up to twenty men and girls at any one time, as well as continuing to carry out heavy preaching commitments and work on the streets at night. Jennifer was shattered and bore most of the weight of the girls' problems. They existed from day to day, never quite knowing where the next meal would come from. The first winter it was the coal that had run out, leaving the entire household without any source of heat. Jennifer had reached breaking point and demanded that Malcolm do something about the problem immediately, before the children died of the cold. Malcolm prayed. As he prayed, the door bell rang, and Jennifer went to answer it. David Carpenter, a friend from St James, Weddington, stood on the doorstep holding a gas fire and said, 'Is this any good to you?' Within ten minutes Malcolm had discovered a redundant gas pipe at the side of the open fire and connected it up. The family said their prayer of thanksgiving huddled around the blissful heat.

In the last year Malcolm had been working closely with a number of local Christians. They supported the work prayerfully and financially, but each of them knew that the time had come for much greater structure and organisation if it was all to be maintained. Malcolm needed strong backing that would release him to continue the work at which he was gifted. He needed administrators, a secretary, a bookkeeper and accountant, legal advisors, a fundraiser, visitors and helpers for the hostels. The list seemed endless, and it all needed to come together as an official body that would give weight and recognition to the whole work.

As always it was important to Malcolm that these people should represent a wide range of denominations. He had no desire for any one church to adopt the project on its own; it had to be a corporate mission involving not only churches but local authorities and government bodies. Everyone has a responsibility towards homeless people, and he was determined to involve as many as he could in the task of bringing their needs before the whole community of Nuneaton. The Council of Churches became his first port of call in search of the backing he needed to continue this important work.

Eleven

Link Up

Guy Cornwall-Jones and David Jameson were both part of the small support group that had emerged over the previous two years. They shared with Malcolm the ecumenical vision for the project and were among the first to recognise the need for a more formal structure. Knowing Nuneaton Council of Churches, they felt it right to warn him that it was not the most exciting or visionary Christian body around. Its numbers and enthusiasm had dwindled over the years, and it had lost much of its sense of purpose and direction in that time. However, if anybody could inspire and motivate people, they were sure it was Malcolm, so they willingly accompanied him to the meeting.

Malcolm delivered his well-prepared speech describing graphically the conditions in which the homeless of Nuneaton lived, sparing few of the painful details. He told them the stories of Duke Street, Midland and Oaston Roads, the miracle of God's provision and the endless stream of men and girls who passed through their doors. He also told them of the ones they were forced to turn away through lack of funds, personnel and space. Finally, without reservation or apology, he asked the council to take the project under its wing, explaining the need for prayer, financial support and volunteers to assist the work. Malcolm made the commitment quite clear, stressing that it was a venture of faith, the future of which was totally in God's hands. If they agreed, he warned them, they'd be embarking on an unknown journey that would cost time, energy and money. He painted a full and realistic picture, hiding nothing.

A stunned silence followed Malcolm's delivery, each member of the council lost for words and hoping that another would be the first to respond. The ice was finally broken by a question; then others slowly started to express interest and concern, one or two even displaying a degree of enthusiasm. An hour or so of discussion followed about exactly what the council could do and how they might go about it. It was an enormous commitment, and while they could see the tremendous need and that God was clearly at the centre of it all, they were still daunted by the responsibility involved. Nobody found the courage to propose outright that they should agree to help; the best they could come up with was a conditional offer. They felt the need for a sign from God, some clear indication that it was right for them to take the project on, especially where the funding was concerned, as their financial resources were limited. Some members of the council left the meeting that night confident that the subject would not be raised again. Others, including Malcolm, went home to wait expecting God to work. Nor did they have to wait long.

Unusually Jennifer was still up when Malcolm got home to Oaston Road, and this time he could see that she was awake with good reason. Far from her usually sleepy state at that time of night, she was pacing around the house smiling all over her face and clutching an envelope in her right hand. He had barely got through the door before she blurted out, 'Malcolm, it's £1,000 more than we've ever received before. Somebody just pushed it through the door tonight with the message 'for your work with the homeless' written on the envelope.' Jennifer had no idea of the details of that evening's meeting until she watched Malcolm go straight to the phone and ring the chairman of Nuneaton Council of Churches. 'We've got our sign,' he said. 'Will £1,000 do for starters?'

Motivation and enthusiasm among the Council of Churches ran high following the 'sign' God had given. They needed that encouragement, as much of the work in the early stages proved boring and tedious. The drawing up of a constitution, appointment of trustees and officers and the forming of a working committee took hours of detailed planning. Registering the association with the Charities Commission involved a solicitor and endless form filling. This lengthy process taught Malcolm a great deal about administration and the need to do things right and in order. Volunteers with a wide range of gifts and abilities came forward at that time and, together with Malcolm, successfully completed important pioneering stages of the association.

'Link Up' was officially launched in March 1976, the name deliberately chosen to describe the aim of the project – the linking together of homeless men and girls with accommodation and people who could care for them. It was also a 'link up' of Christians from all the different denominations in the town. At the end of the first year David Jameson, who had become the first chairman, looked back on all that had been achieved during this time. In his annual report he wrote:

> This year we have necessarily been concerned a great deal with administration. But we must not forget that 'ministry' and 'administration' come from the same root word, which means 'serve'. The purpose of improving the administration and putting it on a more permanent footing is that the personal ministering to people in need may be more effective. The work of Link Up is essentially a personal ministry. It is a matter of people meeting the urgent needs of other people. This is how it started, and this is how it must go on.

In one sense that first annual general meeting was a dream come true for Malcolm. But in another sense he was living every bit of the reality, working around the clock often seven days a week in order to make the dream come true. In less than a year Link Up had acquired offices and appointed a part-time administrator and secretary. For the first time since leaving Lindley Lodge, Malcolm and Jennifer were receiving a regular income paid by the Council of Churches. A network of volunteer workers had been found and trained to support both men and girls in the various dwellings. A strong team of committed Christians made up the group of trustees and working committee. Representatives came from twelve different local churches spanning eight denominations, all keen to pray, support and keep their church members informed. An advisory council made up of five professionals from various supporting agencies was thrilled and delighted to be included in this unusual project. It seemed quite unbelievable, and it had all happened alongside the day-to-day running of Oaston and Midland Roads, which by then had received 21 girls and 49 men respectively during the first year.

The interest in Link Up spread far beyond its workers and supporters as the local press gave wide coverage, including photographs and interviews with Malcolm, Jennifer and some of the girls. Headlines such as *Their Home for the Homeless* and *Church Project Means Another Chance* captured the attention and imaginations of local people and served to inform them about the needs of the homeless living around them. Professionally produced leaflets describing the aims of Link Up were distributed throughout the churches and placed in other strategic places with a view to increasing support. All these and other efforts were not in vain: Link Up emerged as one of Nuneaton's most important charities, whose work was being recognised both by ordinary people in the street and by the highest officials in the local authority. Rotary clubs and other fund-raising charitable organisations, local industries and business people began to show their support through gifts, donations, discounts and sponsorship. Local authority grants were made available for major building repairs, and funding for workers through Manpower Services schemes. Every stone was turned and avenue explored for the sake of the homeless, and the project went from strength to strength.

As the national problem of homeless people grew during the 1970s, many local and central governments were spending huge sums of money keeping the homeless in hotels or bed-and-breakfast establishments. At the same time there were thousands of empty houses, most of them owned by local councils and awaiting demolition. While shelter of some sort was being provided, the real problems were being ignored. Loneliness, isolation, breakdown in family relationships and the general despair among homeless people increased. Link Up emerged as a small but unique organisation, succeeding where other policies and ventures had failed. Some specialists were convinced that the total solution to the problem of homelessness lay in such short-life property schemes as Link Up's. 'Shelter' worker, researcher and author Ron Bailey gave credit to its success in his book *The Homeless and the Empty Houses* (Penguin 1977), commending its non-statutory approach and strong voluntary basis. The strong Christian foundation on which Link Up was built was also unique, but they were only too pleased to share their experience and ideas with any who wished to know. National recognition by an expert in the field was something they had never sought or expected, but it gave them increased courage and confidence to continue the work they had begun.

As the workload increased, Malcolm and Jennifer packed more and more into their days. Being the only full-time employee meant that it was important for Malcolm to attend as many of the official meetings as he could, which often broke into his evening work on the streets. But they were never short of contacts and people to fill the beds. Churches were taking their own initiative, bringing men and girls to them, while the police, social workers and probation officers were almost queuing up in the hope that Malcolm could accommodate one of their hopeless cases.

As well as the homes to oversee there was the running of the offices at the George Eliot Building in

Nuneaton town centre. Pauline Gray and Pat Kirkwood held the fort there as they dealt with an endless stream of callers and telephone enquiries, as well as providing the secretarial back-up for the whole of Link Up. But it didn't end there; what started out as an enquiry and administration centre developed into something much bigger than Malcolm had ever envisaged.

In the first few months, 397 people had called at the office with problems specifically relating to homelessness. Some needed to be accommodated; some were in trouble with the police; others sought advice on various benefits and allowances for clothing, tools etc. In addition, there had been a further 234 visitors, many of whom were volunteering their practical help, prayers and encouragement. A few looked for guidance and counselling on other matters not related to homelessness. It was just the tip of the iceberg, and it became obvious to Malcolm that the workload had to be shared even more widely. One of the most important tasks for him now was the training and equipping of others to work with him.

In an attempt to do this he wrote and produced a manual called 'Link Up Procedure, Law and Policy'. It contained every possible piece of information necessary for helping the homeless, from current law and criminal legal procedures, to where to find secondhand clothing and fill out forms for Link Up residents. All telephone numbers of supportive doctors, hospital staff; probation and social workers and volunteers were listed. This manual thus served as an important training and information document for the volunteer workers. From time to time they would all come together to discuss their various experiences and learn from each other. Malcolm encouraged and assisted wherever he could.

An increasing amount of time was being taken up with various kinds of small group work at the George Eliot Building. Malcolm was already running small groups for alcoholics, drug users and those seeking rehabilitation. It made sense to bring together several people struggling with the same problems rather than spending hours and hours talking with individuals. While he had a fair amount of personal experience to share, he knew that the greatest impact would come from the men themselves. And it was men like Keith Doughty who had that impact.

Meanwhile Jennifer carried the burden of the day-to-day running of Oaston Road. Getting the girls to accept responsibility for their own lives was hard work. Few looked for jobs, and those who had them struggled to get themselves there every day. When they did, it was rarely on time. The many pregnant girls needed basic education on health and diet as well as preparation for the birth of their babies. They were often reluctant to attend antenatal classes, so the bulk of their help came from Jennifer. With no support from friends or family, two of the younger girls pleaded with her to be with them throughout the birth. She was; Jennifer became the mother that so many of them had lacked. She was always there when they needed her, listening, caring, encouraging and supporting. Above all she gave them love.

Under the new Link Up structures Jennifer had also been officially appointed as assistant treasurer, which involved her in hours of bookkeeping late into the night alter Helen and Paul had gone to bed. Life was full, too full, and the strain began to show on the Worsley household. Jennifer had already sought help from a local Anglo-Catholic priest a year earlier. In desperation she begged him to talk Malcolm into slowing down and spending a little more time with her and the children. She was beginning to feel like the last person on his list of needy people – as if she were a single parent herself.

Malcolm had been surprised to see Father David waiting for him one night when he eventually arrived home. They had not always seen eye to eye on their understanding of gospel presentation, and Malcolm felt sure that this priest must have called to get 'converted'. God couldn't have chosen a more appropriate man to humble him as he began to see that this godly man was practising exactly what Malcolm was only pretending to do – love his neighbour *and* his wife! For a while Malcolm had made a concerted effort to take time off but the demands a year later were almost doubled. It finally took a bout of illness and a near fatal accident to make both of them stop and rethink their priorities of work and home, for these had become unhealthily blurred in the last year or so. Fortunately Malcolm was at home when the accident occurred.

Helen was a healthy, active two-year-old who had been walking steadily for some time and, like most small children, loved the adventure of stairs. Oaston Road was a child's paradise with its many doors, rooms and steps, and interior alterations had created a few more than would normally be found in the average family home. On this occasion she escaped from the room where she had been playing happily under the watchful eye of mother and brother. Only seconds later there came a noise rather like cannons firing several shots in close succession. It was the sound of Helen's small body somersaulting downwards, hitting every single step on the tall, narrow staircase as she fell. Jennifer reached the bottom first and screamed for Malcolm, who was somewhere outside in the garden. The two bent over the motionless body. Helen was limp and colourless. Her lips turned purple; and she had stopped breathing. Malcolm instructed Jennifer to send for an ambulance but then stopped her saying, 'No, let's pray.'

With eyes closed and hearts beating fast, they laid their hands on Helen's head and body. Unable to find the words he needed, Malcolm cried and groaned to God in anguish and desperation for his daughter's life. Minutes passed, and neither of them dared to look, in case what they saw confirmed their worst fears. As he knelt in the silence Malcolm sensed an unusual warmth come into his hands, as if he was immersing them in warm water. It felt hotter and hotter, travelling up his arms and into Helen's body. Still with eyes closed he continued to speak to God in his own personal prayer language for several more minutes. It was only the movement in Helen's body that caused him to stop and open his eyes. It was the most beautiful and precious sight he had ever seen before or since. Her eyes were open, little face smiling and cheeks glowing. She sat up and then jumped to her feet, looking at her parents rather blankly and wondering why they were kneeling on the hallway floor. Within seconds Helen ran off to find her toys.

Malcolm and Jennifer were convinced that Helen was a walking miracle and could barely believe what they had just witnessed. But being so close to tragedy made them stop and think about their lifestyle and the pressures upon them as a family. The children were growing up fast. Paul would soon be going to school and Helen to nursery, and their needs and stages in life demanded more structure and routine. Since receiving a regular income and having sold the house on Duke Street they had managed to get a mortgage on a small property in Blackpool, which became their bolt hole on days and occasional weekends off. But this was clearly not enough. Members of the council were also expressing concern for their health and wellbeing. It was obvious that both were in danger of burning themselves out. On an infrequent visit to the doctor at this time, Malcolm was asked if he had any money. Somewhat confused by the question, he said that they had a little. His GP said, 'Fine! Book yourselves a holiday today, and if you are not out of the country by the end of the week I am putting you into hospital!' Four days later the four of them were in Majorca.

The break gave them time to reflect and pray about their commitment to Link Up. Perhaps their dream had been fulfilled? They had been God's instruments in setting up an interdenominational organisation that was meeting the needs of homeless people in Nuneaton. Had their part in it all come to an end. Was their job complete? Maybe it was time to hand over the work to those with different gifts who could take the project a stage further along the road in God's plan? The questions went round and round in their heads for some time before they reached a decision. But when it was finally made, they had a peace and assurance that it was the right one.

As was the case when they left Lindley Lodge, they felt God calling them out again. Where exactly they would go, what they would do and how they would tell the people of Link Up, they didn't know. But it was definitely time to move on.

Twelve

Moving On

It wasn't easy telling the trustees of their decision to leave Link Up. Their time together had been hard work, and they had grown very close as a team. Malcolm and Jennifer felt partly that by leaving they would be breaking up a family. Undoubtedly all would feel a tremendous sense of bereavement. In a way, the situation was eased slightly because David Jameson had announced his intention to finish as chairman only a few weeks earlier, so the wind of change had already begun to blow. But the news still came as a terrible shock to some members of the committee, who had never imagined Link Up without the Worsleys. In their minds the two were inseparable.

Jennifer and Malcolm allowed a suitable lapse of time between the announcement and their departure to enable the committee to fill the gap. They knew the job would need to be advertised and interviews arranged, all of which was new territory for the trustees and would take time. They continued to encourage and support wherever they could, but their tiredness was quite obvious to people now. There had been moments in the last few months when their faith had felt as weak as their bodies, and it was sheer discipline that kept them going. They prayed earnestly that God would provide Link Up with their successors and show them the direction they should take. It was at times like these that Malcolm was grateful for the new structures that had enabled the burden of Link Up to be shared, and he knew that he could now depend on the faith and prayers of a whole group of people.

One area of work he had especially enjoyed pioneering was the support groups for alcoholics. Classified as an alcoholic himself, he felt confident and able to empathise with the sufferers' condition. Withdrawal and rehabilitation had been hard enough for him, even with the restraint of Haverigg and support of his friends at Lindley Lodge, and he still lived with the scars. Malcolm knew the uphill struggle in front of those men and did everything that he could to help them fight their illness. The results from his group work were encouraging. Several had succeeded in giving up their drinking and were in turn supporting others. It was an exciting and challenging venture for Malcolm, one he knew he would be sorry to leave behind. Wherever God guided him, he hoped and prayed to be able to use the lessons and experiences of his past to the full. He waited patiently and was not disappointed.

Langley House Trust is a Christian charitable organisation concerned for the aftercare of ex-prisoners. The trust has many hostels scattered around the country which serve as halfway houses for men coming out of prison. The Lancaster-based hostel was especially concerned for elderly men who remained homeless after their sentences. Many had severe drinking problems, and the trust was looking for someone to pioneer a specialist unit within the hostel for alcoholics. The job came with a reasonable salary and a house. It held the title of warden and was brought to Malcolm's attention by a social worker friend. Following a visit and interview, the trust was delighted to offer him the position. With their house not too far away in Blackpool and easily accessible for weekends off, they felt confident that the move was right. Meanwhile the Link Up trustees had interviewed and appointed Dick and Muriel Bates to take over Malcolm and Jennifer's job. Things seemed to be coming together well, and God was surely answering their prayers.

There were many arrangements to be made for the children, who were now at school and nursery, as well as furniture and belongings to pack. Jennifer was weary and wondered how she was going to cope with the next few weeks' emotional trauma of saying goodbye and moving to Lancaster. Fortunately there were fewer girls at Oaston Road to worry about as two were about to go to Spain on holiday – a gift given them by one of the Link Up prayer partners as a reward for their effort and hard work during the year. But right at the last minute there was a problem. With only a few hours to go before their departure, one of the girls could not be found. Passports, tickets and luggage were waiting, but Sharon was nowhere in sight.

The problem was easily resolved in Malcolm's eye – Jennifer could go in her place. He would have the children and make all the necessary arrangements for moving if she would take the break she so obviously needed. She laughed at the suggestion, knowing full well that she had already packed her summer clothes and passport and taken them to the house in Blackpool. That didn't change Malcolm's mind. Within minutes he was in the car making the two-hour journey to Blackpool with the intention of bringing back all that Jennifer needed for a holiday. Less than six hours later she was on board a bus to Spain, completely disoriented but too exhausted to object. During the journey she spilt a flask of boiling coffee all over her thigh, leaving her with a serious burn. The entire holiday was spent resting in the shade. It was a God-enforced rest that proved vital in preparation for what became a very difficult six months in Lancaster.

The first disappointment came when the house that they had been promised by Langley House Trust turned out to be a small two-bedroomed flat on the top floor of the hostel. Cramped living conditions and the residential work pressures were equal to Oaston Road and to everything they had sought to leave behind Still feeling a little fragile from the last few years and not wanting to create a fuss at the start of their new job, Malcolm and Jennifer moved in and tried to make the best of a difficult situation. But further blows followed when residents burgled them, stealing some of Jennifer's jewellery and her bike. Other items of enormous sentimental value were also taken. Then they discovered that they were not covered by the trust's insurance. All this didn't help them to settle.

Sadly the work with the alcoholics also had its frustrations. Because the vision for a unit had come from the central committee and not from the local working body, Malcolm felt the conflicts between colleagues who had very different ideas about working with the men. Pressures came to bear upon them to pursue an alternative line of work than that they had both felt Malcolm had been employed to do, and so rather than compromise their convictions, they made the very difficult decision to resign. While serving their notice they made arrangements to move to their house in Blackpool and face the future there. How they would pay the mortgage they were not sure.

Frank Rice was the local liaison probation officer for the Langley Trust Hostel. Based in Lancaster, he visited clients there regularly and got to know Malcolm and Jennifer well in that time. He liked Malcolm's ideas and recognised the unique experience and abilities of this man. Hearing of his resignation, Frank arranged for Malcolm to see a colleague who was responsible for setting up a new probation hostel near Blackpool.

Hoole House in Elswick used to be an old isolation hospital surrounded by sixteen acres of beautiful grounds, and Duncan Brown was the senior probation officer responsible for its opening as a probation hostel. Malcolm knew nothing about the man or his ideas for working with men and after the Lancaster experience was naturally cautious about accepting any job lightly. But on this occasion his respect for Frank was sufficient for him to want to pursue it as a possibility. They arranged to meet at Hoole House. Only minutes into their conversation, Duncan looked up at Malcolm and said, 'I'm a committed Christian and I'm looking for a team who will work with me upholding Christian principles. How do you feel about that?' For a few seconds Malcolm was lost for words; not a common problem for him. He quickly recovered, and the two men spent the next few hours exchanging ideas, experiences and exploring the realistic possibility of Malcolm becoming assistant warden for the hostel.

The disappointment of the last six months drifted into the background as the Worsleys made plans to live permanently, for the first time since they had bought it, in their Blackpool house. Jennifer dared not get too excited about the prospect of having a normal family home for the first time in their married life and a husband who went to work like other men, just in case something should go wrong. But this time it didn't, and Malcolm thrived on the challenge and stimulation of working alongside probation officers at Hoole House. They in turn grew to value and appreciate the unique experience and understanding that he had of the men who lived there. In fact the deputy chief of the Lancashire Probation Service was so impressed with Malcolm's work that he invited him to discuss the possibility of full-time training within the probation service.

Harry Rooney was convinced that the Probation Service needed men like Malcolm Worsley and was quite prepared to use his weight and seniority to pave the way for him to be accepted for training. Both men knew that Malcolm's prison record was the only, but enormous, obstacle in the way and a little bit of research revealed that every application from an ex-convict in the past had failed miserably. Malcolm was quite sure that there was no hope; why should his case be considered any different from the others, and there was every chance that his record was much longer than most. But Harry persisted, and, promising his full support and backing, persuaded Malcolm to submit an application for a two-year CQSW course with view to training as a probation officer. He waited for the rejection slip to arrive.

London-franked letters were rare in the Worsley household, least of all those with the Home Office printed on the envelope. The very official-looking document invited him to attend a special interview with the Chief Inspector of Probation in connection with a recent application for training within the probation service. Harry Rooney was the only one not surprised by the news.

Malcolm felt rather numb and, having never expected to get beyond a rejection slip, slightly nervous and daunted at the prospect of an interview at the Home Office. It was with mixed emotions that he travelled down to London, not wanting to build up his hopes, but also fearing what he knew would be a feeling of rejection should he fail to be accepted. God had promised him a future of hope and purpose, but he knew that the promise didn't spare him from these difficult moments when he had to learn to trust.

It was a highly skilled interview, thorough, and with its tense moments. Malcolm had decided to take it slowly and honestly. Even if he had wanted to, there was no way he could outwit these chaps. They'd been interviewing people all their lives. So he sat back and gave the most honest account of his life that he could, which of course included his Christian testimony. But by the time he got on the train home later that day he could recall nothing; his mind had gone blank with sheer exhaustion.

At the end of the longest two weeks of their lives, the second letter from the Home Office eventually arrived. Jennifer and Malcolm both stood staring at it with disbelief. History was in the making: in spite of his criminal record, he had been accepted for social work training with a view to becoming a probation officer. Not only that, but they were prepared to give him a full grant and generous book allowance, plus full expenses for the course. There was also the prospect of a job waiting for him at the end. Malcolm spent the next few weeks thanking God, Harry Rooney, Duncan Brown and Hoole House for making an impossible dream come true.

Studying was no problem to Malcolm. Since prison days he had continued to work at one or another correspondence course and had found great satisfaction in using the brain that had lain dormant for so long. The chance to read and study a subject of which he had so much practical firsthand experience excited him intellectually. But the course was also stimulating practically, calling for several weeks' placement when students were expected to fulfil a wide range of social and probation work practices. A few weeks before they were to go out, the college principal asked to see Malcolm in his office.

'I've been taking a great interest in your work, Malcolm, and I've decided that you are living with a ghost in your life and I want to help you get rid of it.' Malcolm didn't need the statement explained; he was all too aware that he was living with his prison record on his shoulder. It was a psychological battle that had resurfaced when he started college, and he was struggling to get rid of it. He welcomed his tutor's invitation of help but wasn't quite prepared for the suggestion that followed.

'I've arranged for you to do your first-year residential placement at Lancaster Prison, working alongside the probation officer there. It's all cleared with the governor. You've got to go into prison next year as part of your probation office placement, so I suggest you face it now before that time arrives.'

Nervous, but confident that he was going with the backing of the college and the prayers of many people, Malcolm stood outside the forbidding doors of the Lancaster jail. The all-too-familiar bell rang, and a prison officer opened the door. He delivered his well-rehearsed speech:

'I'm Malcolm Worsley, student in training for probation work, and am reporting for placement duty within the prison.' He handed the officer the official college letter verifying his position. It was only when the letter wasn't automatically taken that he looked more closely at the man and read the expression of disbelief and horror in his eyes.

'Why do you say you are here?', the prison officer asked him for the second time, only now with a harsh note in his voice.

'I'm a probation student and have come to work here for the next six weeks,' Malcolm mumbled.

'Not in this bloody prison, you're not,' the man said and slammed the door in his face. It was his landing officer from Walton Prison.

The devastation was indescribable. How he made the journey home to Jennifer and faced the college he didn't know. There were moments in the next few days when he wondered if he would ever recover.

God had used many different people to support Malcolm through the years, but there was no doubt that the members of his college tutor group became his mainstay at this time, both individually and corporately. They sensitively and perceptively led him through the trauma, restoring pride and dignity to his crushed spirit. The prison governor was informed about the incident and later invited him into the prison to receive an apology. Alternative arrangements were made for him to work in a nearby rehabilitation centre for physically handicapped men and women.

Two years came quickly to an end, and the delight of being a fully qualified social worker helped the negative memories of the prison incident to fade into the background. Lancashire Probation Service offered Malcolm a job in its Fleetwood office, just a few miles from their new home in Carleton. With Paul and Helen enjoying their new school and Jennifer finding a part-time teaching job, everything was coming together well for the Worsley household. Malcolm was really beginning to believe that he was 'normal' and could lead a normal life like any other family man. They spent the next ten years doing just that.

Thirteen

The In-between Years

The Old Testament character Joseph had more than a fair share of high drama in life, so much so that he became a good subject for the popular musical *Joseph and his Technicolor Dreamcoat*. Most people are able to recall his colourful coat, dreams, attempted murder, prison sentences and later his rise to power and fame, as well as the dramatic way in which he was restored to his alienated family. But few will remember the details of the years between these two worlds, when he was slowly and steadily growing as a person, rebuilding a shattered life and restoring piece by piece the self-worth and confidence that had been squashed out of him by his jealous and cruel brothers. These were the silent years of growth that made him the man who was able to lead a nation through trauma and crisis and receive lovingly without bitterness or resentment the family who had earlier rejected him. Thousands of years may separate the lives of Joseph and Malcolm, but God's handling of them both in the middle phases of their lives is similar. Neither knew what the future would hold, but both had turned their backs on the past and were determined to move on.

Malcolm had already made enormous strides, far beyond all he could ever have hoped or imagined. But deep inside there were things that he had to prove to himself. Failure still haunted him, and even though he was assured of God's forgiveness, somehow Malcolm couldn't forget. He longed to reconcile parts of his past with the present, bringing healing and wholeness into many relationships and circumstances. Despite the training, qualifications, and the job he now held, nothing would convince him that he was 'normal'. Only time would tell whether he was capable of maintaining a stable, secure lifestyle that fulfilled responsibilities to his wife, children, employers and society. For his own peace of mind he had to succeed where in the past he had failed so miserably.

At work in the Fleetwood office only Malcolm's boss officially knew the details of his past. It was considered unnecessary for everyone on the staff to know, something Malcolm appreciated enormously. It was so important for him to be able to build up good, strong, healthy and 'normal' working relationships without feeling people were either hiding prejudice, making exceptions for him or taking pity on him. He wanted to be accepted and appreciated in his own right, on the basis of his personality now, not in relation to what he had been in the past. Maintaining those relationships over an extended period was critical for him to believe in himself and in his abilities and skills as a probation officer. Working as part of a team, recognising and releasing each other's gifts, was also an important part of this growth process. But he need not have been anxious, for what God had begun he was very definitely going to bring to completion.

Within a short space of time Malcolm had gained the respect and recognition of his colleagues. Not only did he fulfil the work requirements, but he pioneered new ground in his work with young offenders, setting patterns which others would follow. In an attempt to keep these boys and youths out of borstals and detention centres Malcolm developed and led outdoor activity weeks that would challenge them physically, mentally and emotionally. Many discovered depths of character they didn't know they had and which in time gave them the determination and strength needed to keep out of trouble, especially out of prison. Often Malcolm went beyond the bounds of duty, spending additional weekends taking youngsters away on hostel and camping trips up into the Lake District. It became a family activity involving Jennifer and the children, their corporate lives once more influencing those who had little or no experience of family love and security.

In time their joint, relatively high and stable income enabled them to buy a rather small, dilapidated terraced cottage in the Lake District. It needed vast amounts of work before it could be enjoyed to the full, so many weekends were spent knocking parts down and rebuilding. Once more Malcolm's building skills were put to full use. The Waingate cottage became their place of refuge, a holiday home for friends, family and colleagues. It was no surprise to those who knew them to discover that the cottage was in Haverigg, just a few hundred yards from the entrance to the prison drive. Each time they went there, Malcolm pinched himself just to make sure that he wasn't dreaming and that he really was the owner of two properties. God was teaching him how to be that good steward – for which Shirley Marsh had set the example so many years before at Lindley Lodge. Their simple lifestyles had barely changed, but God was teaching them to put their extra earnings to wise use. Their homes were their places of ministry, and many were sent into their lives in this way.

The vicar of the local church where they worshipped in Carleton was one of the few who knew of Malcolm's chequered history. To the average onlooker, especially neighbours, they were simply a lovely friendly young family who worked hard in their professions and homes. Helen and Paul attended the local primary school, and together they worshipped at the village church. Once settled in his new job, Malcolm took up his lay readership, assisting in the leading of worship and occasionally preaching.

Carleton Church was quite different from where he had worshipped previously. The churchmanship was Anglo-Catholic and the style of worship new to him, but he didn't allow that to stop him from becoming a much loved and valued member of the fellowship. Unity between and within the denominations was always one of Malcolm's priorities, and here was a further opportunity for him to display his yearning for oneness in the faith. In an attempt to draw people together, he embraced different spiritual traditions and accommodated varying styles of worship but never moved from his strong stand on personal salvation and new life in Christ. God used him to encourage many m that faith, not least through their fortnightly Bible studies at home and the young people's group. But at no point did he feel free or led by God to give his own powerful testimony and, in contrast to his time in Nuneaton, there were no invitations to go out speaking at other evangelistic rallies and events.

Life took on a very different routine and perspective. Normal working hours released time and space for Malcolm to discover delights he had missed completely in earlier life. Jennifer thrived on their stable family life, enjoying the security of routine, and pursuing her own career as a full-time teacher. She continued to encourage and support Malcolm in his pursuit of 'normality'. From time to time their bungalow would be littered with the evidence of his latest hobby, the phase which most people go through in adolescence but which Malcolm had never entered. One week it would be stamp collecting; the next, playing golf or painting; then photography; and after that bird watching. Each interest would totally absorb his surplus energy as he endeavoured to cram into a few weeks the many years he had lost as an alcoholic and criminal. He followed many of the children's interests with them, strengthening the bonds he had barely felt with his first two sons, Stephen and Alan.

Attending school assemblies, open days, parents' evenings, concerts and standing on the touch line of the local football pitch watching young Paul earn his place in the school team were important events in the process of restoration. God had given him another chance, and Malcolm was a father in the making, learning daily how to love, support and encourage his children. It was so important to him that he gave them his best, all he had and more. His failure with Alan and Stephen still hurt and, ironically, the more he proved to himself that he could now be a responsible parent, the more it pained him that he had let his first two sons down.

There were painful moments when his mind would turn back nearly ten years to a particular day inside

Haverigg Prison. A prison officer had ushered him into the interview room informing him that he had a visitor. The social worker sitting at the desk was unknown to him and quite unexpected. And the news that he gave was an even greater shock: Josephine, Malcolm's first wife, had met another man. They intended to marry, and she wanted Malcolm to sign the adoption forms allowing her new husband to become legal guardian of Alan and Stephen. He had less than half an hour in which to decide. Their divorce had somehow been relatively painless, as Malcolm realised only too well that he couldn't expect Josephine to forgive him for the dreadful things he had done. He knew he had to release her to a new life. But even though he had not seen the two boys for some time, actually sitting there trying to decide whether he should sign them away to another man was already a nightmare. He was their father and always would be; no one could ever alter that fact, but having become a Christian he was also very conscious of his failure as a father.

He wrestled within himself, staring blankly at the social worker whose job it was to get the forms signed. He knew that by not signing he was being selfish. At that time he thought it unlikely that he would ever be in a position to offer them a stable home in which to grow up, but here was a man who could. Bert had been part of Alan and Stephen's lives since they were three- and one-year-old respectively. For their sakes Malcolm began to see the sense in it all, however painful it might be for him.

An added complication was that Bert planned to take them all to South Africa to live, where they would have the chance to get away from the pain of the past and start again. It was unlikely he would ever see them again. He had no way of telling them he loved them, and no way of guaranteeing that his signature on those forms wouldn't be interpreted as 'I don't want you'. Yet nothing could be further from the truth. It was the love of a father that released them to a far better way of life than he could offer at that time. It was love which let them go. It had been one of the hardest things he had ever had to do and was still surfacing painfully ten years later.

Alan and Stephen were never far from Malcolm's thoughts and prayers during these years, but his sense of failure always prevented him from trying to establish contact with them. Even if he had found the courage, he wouldn't have known where to begin finding them. It was therefore quite a shock to discover 'coincidentally' while in casual conversation with friends one day that someone bearing the name of his ex mother-in-law lived very close by in Preston. A nervous 'butterfly' feeling inside him somehow told him that it was undoubtedly Betty. After much thought, prayer and deliberation, he made the decision to ask a good friend to visit Betty and tell her something of Malcolm's life since leaving Haverigg and to ask if he might call to see her. It was more from a state of disbelief, shock and curiosity that she agreed to a meeting than from a genuine desire to see Malcolm, but a time and date was agreed.

The first half hour was awkward and difficult as Betty and Malcolm sat staring at each other in a state of disbelief. He said very little, waiting for her to speak. Gradually she began to bring to the surface the horrific memories of the earlier years of his life. It was a painful period of time, but he knew he had to sit and listen. There were things he himself couldn't remember or perhaps had chosen to forget, but at no point did he try to defend or justify himself. The look on his face and the way in which he sat said it all – 'I'm guilty and deserve nothing.' The visit was the first of several carefully arranged meetings where together they worked through some of the painful times of the past and built a relationship on new ground. It took some time for Betty to adjust to the new Malcolm. She didn't believe in miracles, yet she knew she was looking at one.

As time went on she melted under the warmth and love she was now experiencing in place of the selfishness she had once known in him. They were destined to meet far more frequently than either of them ever expected, as each discovered the other owned a holiday cottage in Haverigg. How - other than God's divine planning they had never bumped into each other in the tiny two-shop village they did not know! A piece of the jigsaw in Malcolm's past had been delicately replaced by his Master Builder, and he walked one more step along the path of wholeness.

It was Betty who restored the link between Malcolm and his sons, her grandsons. Much prayer and thought went into the letters he wrote them in South Africa. He asked for nothing other than an opportunity to explain why he felt he had to sign their adoption papers. Their replies were more than he could have hoped for, especially from Alan, the eldest, who had some very real memories of his father. It was the start of a long process of catching up between father and sons that continues to this day. As married men with families of their own, they were able to understand something of the bonds between parents and children, however far apart they might have been. Those bonds were emotionally renewed just a few years later when Stephen came home to visit his father, Jennifer, Paul and Helen in Carleton. Father and son spent a wonderful few days together walking in the Lake District, getting to know each other and building the foundations for their future relationship.

Malcolm knew that he couldn't undo the past or try to compensate for it but should, as he had done with Betty, work through as much of the past as he could and build on new ground. It was important for his new family that he didn't dwell on the negative details of bygone years but that Alan and Stephen saw him as the man he now was, and were able to receive Jennifer and the children as part and parcel of their father's life. Jennifer had been scared of meeting Malcolm's first two children, not only for herself but for Helen and Paul also. They had some knowledge of their father's past, but not in great detail. In the end she need not have feared. Stephen's departure at the end of his visit was surrounded with tears from everybody, and firm promises were made for both Helen and Paul to visit them in South Africa as soon as the funds could be found. Two years later they spent three wonderful weeks with their half brothers, their wives and families.

Meeting Josephine when she was on holiday with her mother in Preston was not quite such a smooth experience. The hurt inside her went understandably deep and was compounded by the recent breakdown of her second marriage. She had heard about Malcolm's new life, new wife and children from her mother, Betty;

but in many ways this news had intensified her pain and anguish, and their meeting provided her with an opportunity to give vent to many of those feelings. Malcolm stood and took as much as he was able to take, knowing full well that he had no defence. Eventually he walked away, paralysed by the painful knowledge of the deep hurt and pain that he alone had inflicted on one woman. It was some time before he could even pray about that meeting, and he secretly hoped there would not be another.

Josephine's third son, born to her second husband, was called Peter. Following the breakdown of his parents' marriage he had come to live with his grandmother in Preston, spending much of his spare time in Haverigg at one of the other cottages on Waingate. Nobody was more surprised than Malcolm to see him standing at the cottage door one day asking if he might come in and talk. It was the first of many hours spent with Peter in Haverigg as they forged a strong friendship together. Malcolm became the father figure Peter had missed so desperately in the later stages of his growing years. The family circle was widening, and its base was increasingly in Haverigg.

With Peter now living in England permanently, Josephine made regular trips to visit both her son and mother. She had heard about Malcolm's links with Peter, although her next encounter with him had not been planned. Haverigg's main street was not large and without appearing extremely rude one couldn't avoid another person walking by. Malcolm and Josephine met head on. He froze on the spot, hardly daring to breathe for fear of the pain he felt sure he was about to experience. Josephine's eyes were softer and her voice calm as she spoke. 'Thank you for helping my mother, Malcolm, and for spending time with Peter. It's appreciated very much, especially with me being so far away.' To Malcolm they were words of healing and perhaps in God's time and by his grace he might be forgiven by Josephine. He felt he had no right to ask but silently hoped and prayed.

Healing and wholeness in Haverigg was becoming quite a regular feature of the Worsleys' lives during this time. Their cottage was now in full use, and much of their holiday time and weekends were spent there growing together as a family. The probation work in Fleetwood continued to be a challenge and real encouragement to Malcolm. Life was good, fulfilling and very happy. The Worsleys could see no reason why it shouldn't continue that way for the rest of their lives . ..until a passing comment in the staff room during a coffee break stirred up in Malcolm that strange feeling that he had experienced so many times in the past when he was being moved on. But on this occasion it was more like being moved home.

Fourteen

Back to Haverigg

'Hey, Malcolm, there's a job going at Haverigg Prison. Why don't you apply for it? It's just what you need, and you could go and live in your cottage.'

The speaker was one of Malcolm's colleagues, who was sitting on a desk browsing over the job advertisements while drinking coffee. There was no great flash of lightning or clap of thunder with voice from heaven saying, 'Malcolm Worsley, I call you from Fleetwood to the probation department of Haverigg Prison.' Far from it. In fact he can't remember giving his colleague any kind of meaningful reply. He simply grunted something like, 'Oh, really?' But inside a disturbing feeling welled up. For some years he hadn't experienced it, but now it had surfaced again, and he recognised it immediately.

At home later that night he told Jennifer about the job and tested her with the possible thought of applying. 'Do you think Haverigg would have me back as a probation officer?' he asked. Jennifer knew better than to dismiss the impossible where Malcolm was concerned and simply said, 'Well, you could always try. What have you got to lose?' On the surface Malcolm had nothing to lose. He'd got a good job, salary and a healthy family life. Failing to get the Haverigg position wouldn't change any of that. And yet something bothered him deeply. In the likely event of failure, could he take what would undoubtedly be a knock to his pride? And dare he risk bringing to the surface further hurt and pain stemming from his time in Haverigg? These were big questions to be faced before he could even send off for an application form.

Malcolm decided to seek advice, especially from his colleagues, whose opinions he valued greatly. He talked through the realistic possibility of applying for the job with the senior probation officer at Fleetwood, fully expecting her to laugh at the idea. On the contrary, she both encouraged him and promised a good reference. That, together with the wisdom and prayers of Christian friends, gave him the confidence he needed to complete the form. Within a few weeks his references had been taken up, and he was offered an interview.

Ian Lockwood, Haverigg's governor, made no attempt to hide his astonishment on hearing of Malcolm's record. 'I'm sorry, Mr Worsley. If I had known you had a criminal record, you would never have been shortlisted, never mind interviewed. There is no way in my lifetime that the prison service will be so enlightened as to employ an ex-convict as a probation officer. I'm sorry you have been put through this.' It was short and swift. It only took seconds to flatten him. In cricketing terms he was out on a 'no ball'.

The words penetrated deep into Malcolm's spirit. They were everything he had feared, and right then he couldn't understand why God had allowed him to go through it. The disappointment hung over him for weeks. He was hurt, confused and wavering in his faith. Even the suggestion that he should apply for another post with the Cumbria Probation Service (in White-haven) didn't soothe the pain inside. Despite the immediate rejection at Haverigg, one of the assistant chief probation officers responsible for drawing up the short list had seemingly been very impressed with his references and was quite sincere in inviting him to apply for the job in Whitehaven. Eventually he agreed to submit an application and was successful.

The move to Whitehaven helped Malcolm to over-come the disappointment. It was a fresh challenge and opportunity to develop new ideas and friendships. His seven years with Lancashire Probation Service had given him good experience that was to prove invaluable in the days ahead. He lived from Monday to Friday in his Haverigg cottage and travelled home to the family at weekends. It worked well for them as Jennifer was now teaching at a sixth form college, and Helen and Paul were rapidly approaching their examination years. It would have been the wrong time to move the children, but this way the whole family worked long and hard hours during the week and enjoyed their quality time together at weekends.

The early teenage years for Paul and Helen were typical of most. Life was full and active as each of them pursued their own interests and studies. Growth and development in all areas of their lives was plain to see, and the spiritual was clearly part of that. Both had made very definite professions of faith and were eager to grow as Christians. The village church where Malcolm was still lay reader and home group leader included many young people, and he and Jennifer, along with other parents, were actively involved in running both spiritual and recreational activities for them. As time went on, many of the youngsters fell away from the faith to explore other teenage attractions. Those who remained found the reluctance of the church to involve and include them in their services of worship a real struggle and so in determination to carry on in their faith looked elsewhere. Paul and Helen were among them. The local United Reformed Church provided that opportunity. Paul was soon playing his drums and Helen singing, but, more importantly, both found a welcome and acceptance in worship for which they had been searching. So it was with a tinge of sadness that the children began to worship apart from their parents.

Some time later in an attempt to further good strong ecumenical relationships and to be with Helen and Paul, Malcolm and Jennifer made the decision to join them on Sunday evenings. It became the start of a strong friendship with the young URC minister and an opportunity for Malcolm to pick up on some of the interdenominational preaching he had missed in the previous few years.

Invitations to preach at different churches, men's evangelistic events and mid-week meetings started to arrive on his doorstep. God seemed to be opening opportunities once more for Malcolm to preach. For the first time in nearly ten years, God set him free to tell again his testimony of how, where and when he had committed his life to Jesus. It was with anxiety that he stood in the front of his own church and shared his story with the congregation for the very first time. Though initially shocked and a little confused, the majority thanked him warmly for his honesty and faith. The local village policeman shook his hand firmly, expressing respect and friendship for him. A few couldn't get to the door fast enough, and one or two blatantly ignored both him and Jennifer. These were his brothers and sisters in Christ, with whom he had worshipped and served for years. He could only love and pray for those who were struggling and thank God that his testimony had been an encouragement and brought most of them closer together.

A change in the curacy at the church around this time introduced many different ideas and interpretations of liberal Christian teaching. Malcolm had always managed to adjust to different spiritual expressions and styles of worship, but the one thing on which he'd always stood firmly was the authority of scripture as the word of God and the need for a personal relationship with God through salvation and faith in Christ. For the first time ever in his preaching and ministry he felt that he was being asked to compromise on these and other vital matters basic to his faith. He couldn't. So it was with a deep sadness and regret that several months later Malcolm felt obliged to resign his lay readership and leave that particular church. Many, including the wardens, came to express their sadness and love, especially those who had been faithful members of their home group. Malcolm and Jennifer felt bereaved and very much needed the support and fellowship that the United Reformed Church then lovingly offered.

Despite the difficulties at Carleton Church, the team vicar from near by Poulton-le-Fylde, the Reverend Carl Berryman, remained a good friend to Malcolm. He encouraged him to think through the differences in doctrine that were the centre of the problem, and both men learned to respect each other's differences and remain good friends. Some months later, hearing of Malcolm's resignation, a previous curate of Carleton Church, Chris Entwistle, invited him to transfer his lay reader's licence to his church just two miles away in Blackpool.

The cottage on Waingate proved cold in the winter months, and the daily drive to and from Whitehaven both expensive and tiring. It was one of the neighbours who first pointed out the house on Tarn Head, suggesting to Malcolm that it might be a little more comfortable for him and bigger now that Paul and Helen were growing. The garden virtually backed onto the prison grounds. It made a lot of sense, and both Malcolm and Jennifer thought it had great potential. But somehow the Waingate cottage had become part of them as a family, especially as they had spent so many hours rebuilding it. They couldn't bear to sell it. Some of their friends who had spent happy holidays there agreed with them – they couldn't possibly sell it! In a mad moment Malcolm suggested that they should keep it, take out an extra mortgage and still buy Tarn Head. The family laughed at the thought of owning three properties. Malcolm didn't laugh, but he smiled to himself as he remembered saying to Max Wigley back in the police cells at Bradford, 'What! God provide houses? How can God provide me with a house?' He felt sure God was smiling too.

They had no trouble letting Waingate to friends for holidays, and the income somehow always managed to cover the costs. The whole family enjoyed the benefits of Tarn Head, and Malcolm once more embarked upon his next building project. From time to time, the probation work at Whitehaven took him into Haverigg, although he hadn't seen Ian Lockwood since his interview earlier that year. Malcolm had always been concerned for conditions within prisons and, whenever he had an opportunity, had fought for their improvement. He felt sure also that the church had an important role to play, so when he read of a conference taking place at Lincoln run by the Bishop of Lincoln, he was very eager to attend. With a list of international speakers, it was a high-powered conference aimed at senior and chief probation officers, high court judges and prison governors. The numbers were to be restricted to 250. He knew he didn't fit the category at all but was delighted to discover that nobody from the Cumbria Probation Service was attending and that he was therefore, granted permission to go. Sponsored jointly by the Probation Service and his own diocese, he set off to Lincoln full of expectation and enthusiasm. He wasn't disappointed.

Arrival was any time between two and six p.m. Malcolm decided to arrive in good time and so drew up in the large car park at about three. Ian Lockwood pulled up alongside him only seconds later. The two men got out simultaneously. Malcolm smiled knowingly but waited for Ian to break the ice.

'Don't I know you from somewhere?' he asked across the top of his car.

'Yes, you turned me down for a job in your prison earlier this year,' replied Malcolm. 'What are you doing here?' he asked curiously, This is for chief probation officers, and you're not one, are you?' 'No, just an ordinary probation officer,' said Malcolm feeling quite justified in his position, but refusing to volunteer any further explanation. 'Oh,' Ian said, somewhat confused, 'Enjoy the conference.' And he walked off.

Malcolm didn't especially want to engage in deep conversation with the Haverigg governor as he still felt a little sore from the pain of not getting the job. So he was thankful for being able to lose himself among the other 250 or more conference delegates. By the law of averages he thought that he should probably have to see him once or perhaps twice in passing during the three days of the conference. He could just about cope with that as long as it was at a distance.

He relaxed and decided to make the most of this golden opportunity to influence some of the 'powers that be' with his first-hand experience and growing concern for prisons and prisoners. Much to his horror that very evening he came face to face with Ian Lockwood again, at dinner. Without realising it, the governor had taken a seat directly opposite Malcolm. They made polite conversation. During the next two days, by some sheer fluke, or, as Malcolm began to sense, divine planning, they found themselves placed in the same discussion groups. He tried to ignore Ian and carry on as normal, but it was difficult not knowing quite what game God was playing!

The three days passed quickly, an invaluable time of learning and contributing. The final meal together was Sunday lunch. On this occasion Ian Lockwood deliberately sought Malcolm out. He was warm and encouraging as he said, 'Malcolm, it's been good to get to know you these past few days. I like your ideas, and want you to work in my prison. Will you apply if a suitable post becomes vacant?' This was no time to bear grudges, and Malcolm heard himself say, 'Yes, I'd love to as long as I'm not 'out on a no ball' this time!'

Only days later Haverigg's governor telephoned to make Malcolm aware that a probation officer's post was available within the prison. He had spent the last few days clearing the matter with the Home Office and the Prison Officers' Association. The latter was given 48 hours in which to put any objections in writing. No one did. Naturally normal procedures were followed, and he found that he was short-listed along with a friend and colleague from the local office in Barrow. In the event Malcolm was offered and accepted the position, agreeing to start within a month.

History was made. Never before or to his knowledge since has an ex-prisoner been appointed as a probation officer to the same prison in which he had served his sentence. Several people on the staff remained from the days when Malcolm was an inmate. One was a teacher who had always been a great encouragement to him and was delighted to see him back in his present capacity. Another was a prison officer whose job it now was to give Malcolm his keys to the prison. It went against everything that this man had ever been taught to do. A prison officer never gives keys to a prisoner. It took him two whole days to work through the trauma and resolve his crisis of identity. Having done so he handed over what would give Malcolm Worsley freedom of access to every part of Haverigg Prison. As he took the keys he knew that nowhere here or anywhere else could ever be out of bounds again. The circle was complete.

Fifteen

Promotion

The routine of living at Tarn Head from Monday to Friday and travelling home at weekends to be with Jennifer and the children continued throughout the three year period that Malcolm worked at the prison. It was a very fulfilling and satisfying time in his professional working life. He was keen to put his unique experience to good use in helping others to face the many hurdles and stigmas that he himself had had to overcome. It also became a timely opportunity to put into practise his own theories and ideas that had been slowly evolving over the first five years of his career. The many hours spent working in the field of counselling and group work had provided valuable experience helping him to expand his thinking on the principles and practice of supporting people through times of need and crisis. Slowly but steadily he grew in confidence, skill, and a passion to see damaged and broken lives restored. And there were plenty of those to be found inside Haverigg Prison.

Malcolm was not content to simply do his own job well. He was eager to create structures and resources that would influence the work of the whole prison structure and all personnel engaged in the rehabilitation process of offenders. Team work had been a strong feature of his previous working situations and the structures at Haverigg encouraged a high degree of co-operation and interdependence between its workers. His relationship with one particular colleague, Mark Quigley, worked especially well and together they set about producing a programme that would help offenders come to terms with their guilt, and work towards rebuilding their lives. It was a multi-disciplinary approach that embraced an important spiritual dimension. In addition to the normal areas covered on the path towards rehabilitation they also made available the advice and counsel of priest or other minister of Christian religion. The concept of forgiveness, in spiritual terms, was approached clearly and unapologetically. It proved a helpful and successful programme used repeatedly within the prison.

Counselling was not a skill that Malcolm restricted to use within his working hours. He had become a compassionate listener to many people, whether a client, colleague or friend. Many of his evenings in Tarn Head would be spent listening, sharing and praying with the ever increasing number of individuals who had somehow been put into contact with him. Some were Christians in need of support or encouragement whilst others were, as he himself had once been, damaged individuals in search of a healing, hope and a purpose to their lives. Nothing delighted him more on those occasions than to be able to share his own story of faith – the journey which had brought him from the depths of despair to a place of peace and restoration with God. There were many times when he was privileged to lead people in those first steps of reconciliation with that same God of healing and forgiveness. The freedom he found in his evening work in being able to talk and pray openly with his friends was releasing within him a fervent desire to lead more and more people to a faith in Christ. The opportunity to do just that came sooner than he thought but it was not without a battle.

Long nightly telephone calls to Jennifer and the children were a regular feature of their midweek routine. Each took their turn to offload the days events and concerns. This particular evening Malcolm had a lot to tell. A very interesting position for a senior probation officer had come up in the Lake District town of Kendal. It was just the level of promotion that he had been looking for; specialising in a field in which he knew he had a lot to offer. He felt certain that the few years at Haverigg had been good grooming for seniority. The prospects of the Kendal job were exciting, challenging and offered the added bonus of a considerably higher salary.

There have been very few occasions in life when Malcolm can honestly say he has heard a voice from God. Those moments inside his cell over twenty five years earlier had been one such time and this particular evening turned out to be a second. He was actually in mid-sentence when the voice said, 'You're not going to get that job and I am leading you out of probation work'. The impact was so great that he stopped talking to Jennifer immediately and, without offering her an explanation for his extraordinary behaviour, placed the receiver down. Malcolm stormed out into the garden at Tarn Head and paced up and down the lawn. If it hadn't been for his quick and violent reaction he might have persuaded himself that the voice had been a figment of his imagination. But the message remained crystal clear; quite unmistakable. It was as if the speaker had been standing along side him. He fumed with anger, hurtling angry questions towards the sender. Why shouldn't he go for the job? Didn't he deserve the status of a senior position and recognition before his colleagues? Hadn't he been hard working and faithful, committed and successful in all that he'd done within the prison? Surely, he had earned the right to at least apply for such a position? Why shouldn't he be rewarded with the sense of achievement, professional acknowledgement, top job security and a bigger salary? The one way conversation and striding up and down the lawn continued for some time. Even when the questions eventually dried up his anger did not abate. It had been a long time since he had experienced such depth of feeling about something he wanted to do, and a clear instruction not to go in that direction, was not what he wanted to hear. He felt cheated by God, let down at a time which, in his opinion, should have been the peak of his reward for hard work and dedication. Life had become very comfortable, fulfilling and successful. And Malcolm liked it that way. Why, he wondered, after all he'd gone through and achieved was God turning it all upside down again? If promotion wasn't what God had in mind, what was?

Jennifer was never surprised when Malcolm announced that change was in the air. It had become a regular feature of their somewhat unusual lifestyle over their sixteen years of marriage. But what she couldn't cope with on this occasion, was his state of uncertainty surrounding exactly what that change might be. It was she who suggested he take a few days out in order to think and pray about the future. Kirby Stephen was a small, sleepy Cumbrian town close by to Appleby, and home of a Christian organisation called Maranatha Ministries. Malcolm had seen their advertisements offering short strategy breaks for Christian men and women in search of time and space away from the pressures of every day life. Despite the fact that he had his own quiet cottage and relatives just down the road from Appleby, Malcolm decided to book into Maranatha's small retreat house. He was desperate to hear God's voice concerning the future and prayed fervently that this time away would give him a real sense of God's purpose and direction. By the end of his few days there, he had been offered a job in full time evangelism.

Maranatha Ministries had been receiving more invitations from groups and churches than their full time evangelist Derek Cook could handle. The executive committee took the very big step of deciding to employ a second evangelist. Following prayer and discussion one of its members was absolutely convinced that the job should not be advertised, but the person whom God was preparing for that ministry, would be very clearly sent to them. The decision to wait, trusting in God, had been made a short time before Malcolm's arrival at Maranatha. Over the course of the four days he spent there Derek Cook became increasingly convinced that he was God's man for the job.

It took longer for Malcolm to share that conviction. Giving up a secure, recognised and lucrative position within the prison in order to work for a small, comparatively insignificant Christian organisation for less than half the salary, was not a decision he could make lightly. At one level it appeared ludicrous, and yet at another, it was everything he had ever wanted to have the opportunity to do. He left Maranatha feeling unsettled. It was the kind of restlessness he had experienced several times previously in his life when major change was about to take place. But before he could be sure that this was the right way forward he had to put it through the testing fires.

The opinion and advice of praying friends was very important to Malcolm. He was still in regular contact with many who had supported him through difficult times twenty or more years earlier, and it was often these people he turned to at such crucial moments of his life. That weekend he telephoned several of them, as well as seeking the advice of Christian friends in the Blackpool area, all of whom were conveniently taking part in a march of witness in the town centre that very Saturday morning. Before setting off to join the procession Malcolm remembers telling Jennifer, 'If only one of those people this morning say it's a daft idea, I shan't do it' The only surprise reaction Malcolm received was that such a change in direction should have taken so long. Much to his disappointment, he failed to find any objectors.

The matter was further confirmed that following Sunday evening when listening to a sermon based on the Old Testament story of Ruth. The preacher emphasised the fact that God very often calls men and women out of their secure and comfortable circumstances to serve him in a new and foreign land. It was a timely word for a man who was becoming increasingly convinced that Maranatha was the direction in which he should be walking. There were still however questions in his mind that needed to be resolved, areas that he knew he had to think through before he could finally hand in his resignation to the prison. A week's holiday in Tenerife helped him to do just that. With just £100 in his pocket Malcolm visited the local travel agent and asked for a late booking. That same evening he flew into the Canary Island on a half board package deal costing £99. It was members of the South Tenerife Christian Fellowship in Los Christianos who helped him on this occasion. Peggy and Arnold Maughan spent time listening, reflecting and praying with Malcolm throughout the week. They introduced him to Mairi Lack, a regular island visitor with a very special ministry in prayer. An Anglican priest, Revd. Ian Watts serving in the local English speaking Anglican Church also played an important part in helping Malcolm face some of the consequences of this serious change in direction. Once again God had guided Malcolm through the wisdom, prayers and encouragement of his people. By the time he left, there was no doubt in his mind that to delay the handing in of his notice to Haverigg Prison a day longer would have been to deliberately disobey God's call upon his life at that time.

The Maranatha team was small but their mission field nationwide. Whilst now based in his Carleton home and with the backing of the office in Kirby Malcolm travelled hundreds of miles speaking, preaching, and helping churches and organisations in their ministry of evangelism. Much of the work was undertaken on his own although he always welcomed those times when , especially at weekends, Jennifer was able to join him. Preaching and teaching were undoubtedly the most sought after skills but Malcolm's counselling experience did not go to waste. It was during this period that a group of professional Christian people became concerned to set up an association that would serve as an accrediting body for Christians wishing to achieve high standards of training and competence in counselling equal to that in the secular world. It was a subject very close to Malcolm's own heart and he was particularly delighted to see the birth of what became known as the Association of Christian Counsellors. Knowing of their concern for high standards of training Malcolm sent the A.C.C. a copy of the course that he and Mark Quigley had produced for the prison. He had already successfully used the material with a group of Christian ministers before leaving Haverigg. They had requested the course having recognised the limitations of their own training in handling an increasing number of complex pastoral cases in their churches. Malcolm had been delighted to be able to respond to the need of a group of people who were at the front line of caring in the Christian church and suspected that there were many more who might benefit from such training. The A.C.C. gave their full backing to the course and especially welcomed Malcolm's experience of training in the secular world. He became one of their first members of the board of directors.

With the encouragement and support of the A.C.C. Malcolm made his training courses for Christians seeking professional training and credibility in their work more widely available . Maranatha welcomed this new branch to their ministry and opened the doors of their retreat house to the very first student counsellors. The training given was thorough, of a high standard, acceptable both in the secular and professional world and gave a fresh confidence to an area of ministry that was in danger of being clouded by well meaning but unqualified workers.

Over the following two year period an increasing amount of Malcolm's time was spent preparing, leading and teaching his counselling courses. As the demand grew, he responded by taking them out of Kirby Stephen into churches and areas where they were being requested. Many who had completed the introduction to Christian counselling asked for further training and so more advanced and specialised courses emerged. The spheres of sexual abuse and addiction emerged as particularly needy areas, in which students had found very little previous support or training given. Malcolm's personal and professional expertise were put to full use in developing new material to meet these demands. Whilst the evangelistic preaching and teaching never stopped it became clear that the counselling was a huge mission field in in itself and one in great need of workers. Malcolm always found it hard to separate the two spheres in his own mind. As far as he could see the ministry of counselling was evangelism and the two were intrinsically linked in the redeeming message of the gospel.

With Malcolm as a full time member of the Maranatha staff team Derek and Lillian Cook were able, for the first time, to take a much needed six month sabbatical break from their work, leaving him to hold the fort in their absence. It was during this period that Malcolm became increasingly convinced that he should develop more fully his ministry in counselling care and training. It seemed a very natural step to take and one that had the full endorsement and backing of Derek and Lillian Cook on their return from sabbatical.

Malcolm's time with Maranatha had been an important stepping stone between the security of full time employment in the prison service and what now was clearly emerging as a brand new venture of faith. It had provided the all-important framework while allowing him the freedom to develop his many gifts in evangelistic preaching and teaching as well as pioneer important work in counselling training. But God was moving him on and he knew that it was time to take what felt like a leap in faith. With Jennifer's full backing Malcolm set up his office in the family's back dinning room and began laying the foundations of what became known as The Philipppi Trust.

On 7 January 1993 The Philippi Trust gained full recognition and status as a charity from the Charity Commissioners. Just two days later the trustees held their first meeting at which they officially appointed Malcolm as director and Joyce Mallinson as secretary. It was a day of great rejoicing and celebration. Twelve very different people were united in a corporate vision to see God at work through a ministry of evangelism and counselling. Each had come from vastly different Church backgrounds, occupations and areas of the country. They included ministers from different Christian denominations, a solicitor, doctor, teacher, house wife, chemist, manager and the chairman, Mike Rees, working full time as a probation officer. The first meeting ended with a time of celebration in acknowledgement of the official launch of The Philippi Trust. To mark the occasion Malcolm invited Noel Fellowes, Development Director of the Prison Fellowship, to speak to them. Noel's choice of Bible reading for that evening confirmed in the hearts of everyone present

Philippi's combined ministry of both Christian Counselling and Evangelism. The words of the Old Testament prophet Isaiah spoke powerfully of the dual task that Malcolm himself increasingly felt called to: ' . . . the Lord has anointed me to preach good news to the poor. He has sent me to bind up the broken-hearted ... to comfort all who mourn and provide for those who grieve ... to bestow on them a crown of beauty instead of ashes, the oil of gladness instead of mourning, and a garment of praise instead of a spirit of despair ... '

It was the start of a year packed with evangelistic missions, training and counselling involving thousands of miles travel and many weeks away from home. Invitations flooded into the office and Joyce's invaluable presence at the end of the phone, behind a desk and fingers at the typewriter became an indispensable part of Philippi's ministry. The numbers of individuals committed to praying and giving towards the ever expanding vision also increased. Regular newsletter and prayer diaries were posted to all ends of the country and some even overseas. Malcolm's links in Tenerife not only provided valuable prayer support but became one of the first fellowships to benefit from his extended ministry in teaching and counselling training. This small international link was no surprise to one of the trustees, Dr Mairi Lack, whom Malcolm had met in Tenerife. From the very beginning of her involvement with the trust she had felt a very deep conviction that Philippi's mission field would extend worldwide.

The funds to meet the costs and to supply both Malcolm and Joyce with small salaries came in through faithful praying partners but it became evident that far greater resources were going to be required if the work of Philippi Trust was to meet the rapidly increasing demands being made upon it. The Worsley's Carleton house had become the base for an office, counselling rooms, overnight guest house and occasionally home for Malcolm, Jennifer and the the family! Computers, a photocopier, additional desks, fax machine, filing cabinets and training manuals occupied every available space. During term time Helen and Paul were away at university and Jennifer continued to teach at the local sixth form college but conditions became severely cramped during the teenagers weekend visits and end of term breaks. Within just six months of the official launch of the trust the need for premises became urgent. Prayer partners were urged to place the needs of the work before God and his response came far quicker than any of them expected.

Malcolm's long term vision had always been for a base that could provide ample office space, a number of small and comfortable counselling rooms, a teaching room, plus residential accommodation for several people at any one time who might be in need of intensive care or simply space away from the pressures of their every day life. The staff team had already increased to include Dave Linington, a gifted teacher and experienced Christian counsellor, on a part-time basis. As well as sharing the teaching on the counselling courses and taking on some of the increasing case-load, Dave became Philippi's Development Director. One of his first tasks was to literally develop number 34, Sherbourne Road, Blackpool . The very run down ten-bedroom Blackpool hotel just five minutes' walk from the sea front had enormous potential. An initial gift of £10,000 towards the cost of purchasing it in-

creased the faith and spirits of everyone and the remainder followed in smaller donations. The final miracle
came in the acceptance of an offer on the property some
£27,000 below the asking price. Just ten months after
the official launch of The Philippi Trust, Malcolm,
Joyce, Dave and an ever increasing band of volunteers
moved into two of the 10 rooms in Philippi House. It
became Dave's task to transform it into a fully modern-
ised, refurbished residential centre. It took just fourteen
months during which time the Trust's work expanded
beyond belief.

Invitations for Malcolm to speak to professional
groups, churches, Christian organisations and even in
prisons flooded in. He led missions in London, Slough,
Reading, Northern Ireland and became an associate
evangelist with both the Church Pastoral Aid Society
and The Archbishop's Springboard Commission. He
was also the recipient of the prestigious Cuthbert Bardsley Award in Evangelism. The £1000 cheque was
given in memory of the late Bishop of Coventry and
recognition of Malcolm's exceptional contribution to
the field of evangelism. It was especially meaningful
to Malcolm because of the encouragement that Cuthbert Bardsley had given him personally during his time
working in the Midlands area.

In addition to the evangelism side to the trust's work
literally hundreds of students were enrolled in the counselling courses all over the country. As increasing
numbers qualified at foundation and advanced level, so
Malcolm saw the need to supply ongoing supervision
to them as a support for their ministry. Accountability
was a very important part of the code of ethics laid
down by the A.C.C. and an area that Malcolm felt very

strongly about. Whilst he never stopped teaching and training, his role was clearly expanding and so he welcomed the appointment of full-time staff member, Jan Younger, late in 1994. With a background and training in education Jan was able to take on much of the administration and promotion of the counselling courses as well as share in the teaching.

Meanwhile the office back up team had increased to three part-timers, plus numerous volunteers who came to man the phones, make the tea, clean the offices, paint, decorate or rebuild a room or two as the refurbishment continued. Individual requests for counselling arrived on a weekly basis and so a team of associate counsellors were brought together in order to meet this need both from the Blackpool base and in other parts of the country. It was the start of Malcolm's vision to see the church equipped with trained, competent counsellors from within their Christian community.

Fortunately the completion of the refurbishment programme came twelve months ahead of schedule, exactly two years after the official launch of the trust. On this occasion it was The Rt Reverend Alan Chesters, Bishop of Blackburn, who led the staff, trustees and friends in prayers for the future blessing of all the work at Philippi House. The atmosphere was charged with a spirit of thanksgiving and amazement for all that God had done within such a short space of time. In the words of St Paul in his letter to the Ephesians God had done 'immeasurably more than all we ask or imagine'.

Sixteen

The Road to Ordination

On the morning of 29 June 1996 The Rt. Reverend Alan Chesters, Bishop of Blackburn declared before a full congregation the requirements and duties of those called to be deacons in the Church of England:

> A deacon is called to serve the Church of God, and to work with its members in caring for the poor, the needy, the sick, and all who are in trouble. He is to strengthen the faithful, search out the careless and the indifferent, and to preach the word of God in the place to which he is licensed. A deacon assists the priest under whom he serves, in leading the worship of the people, especially in the administration of the Holy Communion. He may baptise when required to do so. It is his general duty to do such pastoral work as is entrusted to him.

Blackburn Cathedral was packed with the friends, family and supporting congregations of eight nervous ordinands, all of whom had been tried, tested, approved and selected in preparation for this all-important day. Malcolm Worsley was one of them. Unlike the majority of his fellow candidates he was older in years, had been trained on a part-time basis and had qualified for a non-stipendiary ministry. Where others would be paid for their full-time service in their assigned parish Malcolm's duties would be to assist at Sunday services locally whilst continuing to minister in the wider Church during the week through the work of The Philippi Trust. In practical outward terms, he knew that ordination would make only a small difference to his daily work routine but inwardly it was an enormous landmark in a spiritual journey.

The bishop directed the first of seven important questions to the candidates: 'Do you believe, so far as you know your own heart, that God has called you to the office and work of a deacon in his Church.?' Malcolm, along with the others, replied, 'I believe that God has called me.' The calling was sure. He had plenty of anxieties about the legalities, pomp and ceremony surrounding the occasion but there was no doubt in his mind that God had called him to this moment in time. It was a calling to be set apart, not in any sense of importance or elevation, but set apart to serve. It was a calling of submission to God's will and purposes for his life; a calling to become more completely the person that God had created him to be. It was neither the beginning nor the end of a journey, but an important marker along the way. It enabled him to look back with a humble heart and deep gratitude for all that God had done in his life, as well as, look forward to a future committed to bringing healing and hope to those whose lives had been damaged and broken.

The road to ordination had been long and drawn out, starting some ten or more years earlier when one or two friends had suggested quite independently of each other that Malcolm ought to pursue the possibility of 'full time' Christian service. They thought ordination might well be a likely path. At that time he was still working in probation and even though the Home Office had been persuaded, he considered it highly unlikely that the Church of England would consider a man with a criminal record. Malcolm decided to talk the matter through with his friend and priest, Canon Carl Berryman. Carl's reservations were not at all related to Malcolm's record. The principle hurdles, as he saw them, were first the fact that he had been divorced some twenty or more years earlier, prior to his conversion, and second that his experience of the 'Church' had been, in theological terms, a limited one. A visit to the Deputy Diocesan Director of Ordinands confirmed Carl's reservations exactly. Even if the Church of England changed their views on ordaining divorcees, he considered Malcolm's evangelical persuasions far too narrow for anyone entering ordained ministry.

It was several years later, following a third visit to the Director of Ordinands, that the suggestion of a selection conference for ordination was made to Malcolm. In the interim period God had led him into full-time service through Maranatha Ministries and now Philippi Trust. But this further step forward towards ordination was initiated, on this occasion, by two bishops. The suffragan Bishop of Lancaster raised the subject during a meeting with Malcolm concerning a completely different matter and then proceeded to make arrangements for him to see the diocesan Bishop of Blackburn. Just three months later, with the ruling on ordaining divorcees having changed, he had been recommended for training with the Carlisle Diocesan Training Institute.

Part-time theological training enables its students to continue working in their day time jobs and gain much of their practical training at a local church level where they are known, loved and supported. Particularly valued by married students with families, it avoids the upheaval of moving, and considerably reduces the costs compared to full-time residential training. Over a two-year period, Malcolm was expected to allocate up to 15 hours to private study a week, to attend fortnightly seminars, plus six residential weekends and a ten day summer school each year. He welcomed the discipline of study, something he'd always tried to maintain in his Christian life and this particular course turned out to be stimulating. His fellow students were from widely differing church and theological backgrounds providing a microcosm of the Church of England and creating lively and enlightening debate. St Christopher's, Marton, Blackpool became Malcolm's placement church throughout his training, where he served as many Sundays as he was able alongside the vicar, Revd Graham Rainford. As a church of Anglo-Catholic tradition it provided the breadth of experience and understanding that he previously lacked. Malcolm felt loved and accepted by the congregation and looked forward to his future ministry as a non-stipendiary curate.

Preparation for ordination had challenged him at every level. The theological training covered many difficult and controversial issues of the day, some of which Malcolm would have been happier to have skimmed over lightly. But discussions and essays demanded hours of background reading, detailed study of scripture, prayerful heart searching and courage to stand his ground against a wave of alternative opinion. Strenuous though it was, he emerged far better equipped and stronger in both understanding and conviction as a result of the time and effort ploughed into his studies. But preparation at an academic level was just one area covered by ordination training. The spiritual demands were equally taxing.

In being set apart by God for a ministry that would be recognised in the eyes of the Church as serious, responsible and accountable, Malcolm knew that he had a responsibility to carefully examine his inner spiritual world. He tried to bring his own heart and life under God's microscope and face those areas of his character and personality that were in need God's refining. He knew it was a process that was ongoing, a lifetime task that faced every Christian; but as he approached this critical time of commitment to ordination, the responsibility felt greater. God's refining fires were not new to him. His whole life had required restoration, in body, mind and spirit. His experience of healing and wholeness had been one that had stretched over many years and taken many different forms ... Malcolm had grown to recognise God's seasons of healing and come to trust the One who knows him best of all. Sometimes storms had raged with buffeting winds, torrential downpours and penetrating cold as his life was taken, shaken, pummelled and scoured by his creator. At other times the soft dew, gentle breeze and warm sunshine soothed, cradled and comforted. There had been moments when the healing process had been fast and dramatic, the fruits of which were very clear and obvious to onlookers but more often than not it was a slow painful process accompanied with anguish and tears as he learnt to walk step by step in obedience to God's leading. God had been both gracious and gentle and yet uncompromising and demanding. Only as he looked back could Malcolm see the open wounds gradually close and scars slowly fade.

God had used a variety of people, places and situations in the process of rebuilding this life. Not all were welcomed by him and some were consciously and deliberately avoided, or at least battled with. Sometimes he deliberately clung onto wounds of the past, holding them out as reasons and excuses for not moving on in his journey with God. Malcolm told God over and over again that no-one with his background of alcoholism, crime and broken relationships could possibly be considered for ordination. But God refused to listen, reminding him that the past was gone and that he was a new creation. He knew that God had buried the past long ago on the cross of Christ but there was something that occasionally pulled him down inside and made him look back in a negative, destructive way. He found himself raking up what God had clearly dealt with once and for all.

On one particular occasion this became very obvious to a member of church at which Malcolm had been leading a conference. Hazel Barton knew very little about the preacher that day and was not someone used to receiving unexpected 'words' from God but as she sat listening to Malcolm's sermon she felt compelled to record what she could only explain as a message for Malcolm from God. It read; 'I have this servant: saved, renewed, transformed, filled with My Spirit, born again he travels the world telling forth My Word, bringing comfort to the sorrowing, encouraging the weak, feeding the babes with milk, offering cups of cold water, telling the folk of My Love. In his possession is a treasure chest, filled with wonderful miracles of all sizes, quantities of Grace, Joy and Love which I have showered upon him, precious Truths which we have shared together and a hundred other things we have collected since the day he was 'born' in that prison cell. There is something which is a mystery, though: he also possesses a rucksack into which he is always looking, scratching around, turning over the contents and from time to time pulling out of it things I don't recognise, which he shares with the people around him and then stuffs back into the rucksack. Something he shared the other day had the words ... "God reminded me of my past ..." attached to it. He has no "past" in my memory – I have put it as far as the East is from the West why does he like to carry this bag full of the past around so much? I can see it makes him weary and sometimes oppressed. Next time he puts it down I will remove it from his sight so that as he continues his journey he will have no weight on his back but a new lightness in his skip and a new joy in his heart and then the only thing he will have to show from will be "our treasure chest" which is full of wonderful experiences, answered prayers, beautiful friendships, hundreds of miracles, quantities of forgiveness, grace, joy and love, and My Word which will be a never ending source of light and power to my servant and those he meets along the way ...'

Malcolm recognised himself immediately in these painful but beautiful words. They spoke clearly of the inner battle he had been experiencing but, at the same time, provided the assurance and confidence he needed to let go of the heavy weights dragging him down. They were timely words. He was desperate to move on with God. To stand still in the path of growth would be to limit God's work in him, and consequently restrict just how much he could be of help to others. And that he couldn't possibly do.

Since working with the Philippi Trust, Malcolm had uncovered the tip of an iceberg that required skilful and professional defrosting. Hundreds of Christians, many of whom were in leadership, had sought help and support. Many more, yet to find faith, were searching for hope and healing. The small beginnings in Blackpool had now stretched as far as Truro and Tenerife where Philippi House satellites have developed (In recent months requests from Namibia, Rumania, Germany and South Africa have also been made). Malcolm knew that his heart and life are committed to bringing Good News to hurting people, and if ordination was part of God's plan to further that mission, he welcomed it.

Among the friends who witnessed that huge step of commitment on June 29, 1996 were three of the many who had played a huge part directing Malcolm's journey thirty years earlier. As ordained men themselves each of them understood the enormity of the step he was about to take. Canon Max Wigley had been the first to speak to Malcolm of God's transforming love, giving him a copy of the New Testament and writing faithfully to him during his time in Haverigg. Canon John Moore, head of the community at Lindley Lodge at the time when Malcolm had been released from prison, offered him a new family of Christian people who loved and cherished him as a babe in Christ. And Canon Guy Cornwall-Jones was one of the first to encourage and support Malcolm in his early ministry of evangelism upon leaving Lindley Lodge. Among the heavenly cloud of witnesses present that day was the gracious

and loving Scripture Union prison visitor, Will Barker,
who loved and nurtured Malcolm through his prison
days; also Dr Mairi Lack, whom God had taken only a
few weeks earlier. Others in the congregation represented his days working as a probation officer, and, of
course, the ever increasing members of staff, trustees
and friends of Philippi Trust stood united in support.

The hymn, 'Just as I am', put into words, everything
he wanted to express to God:

> Just as I am, without one plea
> But that thy blood was shed for me,
> And that thou bid'st me come to thee,
> O Lamb of God, I come.

> Just as I am, though tossed about
> With many a conflict, many a doubt,
> Fightings within, and fears without,
> O lamb of God, I come.

> Just as I am, poor, wretched, blind;
> Sight, riches, healing of the mind,
> Yea, all I need, in thee I find,
> O Lamb of God, I come.

Malcolm first 'came' to God over thirty years earlier in
his prison cell. His commitment to ordination was an
important landmark in his spiritual growth; a powerful
testimony to God's grace, forgiveness, healing and
redeeming love. This remarkable journey is ongoing.
The destination is certain, but the route decided by God
alone. One thing can be guaranteed – many will discover that same grace, forgiveness, healing and
redeeming love – because of Malcolm's willingness to
share all he has received from God.